DIVORCE

and

The Myth of Lawyers

by

LENARD MARLOW, J. D.

HARLAN PRESS
GARDEN CITY, NEW YORK

Library of Congress Catalog Card Number: 92-071230

International Standard Book Number: 0-9632741-0-4

Published in the United States of America.

To Marilyn,
My wife and loyal supporter.

CONTENTS

ACKNOWLEDGEMENT

This is to acknowledge my appreciation to my good friend Barbara Badolato, who painstakingly read and re-read every chapter in the book and made invaluable suggestions, and to my editor Nancy Papritz, who thoughtfully and generously gave of herself in helping to bring it to life.

Lawyers do not know what is best for us.
Nor are they necessarily wise.
They are just people who went to law school.

PREFACE

People do not get married to get divorced. Their divorce thus represents a great disappointment to them. In fact, it is this disappointment, and the hurt, anger, fear and sometimes sense of betrayal with which one or both of them is struggling, that makes their divorce so painful. It is for this reason that, next to the death of a child or someone else extremely close, divorce is probably the most difficult experience that people will encounter in their lives. To add to the problem, it will take a considerable period of time, and sometimes several years, before one or both of them will be able to come to terms with what it is that their divorce represents.

What people need at this time is help. Help to better understand the difficult feelings with which they are struggling and with which they are so overwhelmed. Help to address and to resolve the practical problems with which they now find themselves faced. And help to enable them, and the immediate members of their family, to come to terms with what has happened to them and to get on with the necessary business of their lives.

Unfortunately, when faced with the tragedy of their divorce, people do not usually turn for help. Instead, they turn to lawyers. Moreover, they will be encouraged by their cadre of advisors that this is what they must do.

Lawyers will not make it better, however. On the contrary, they will only make it worse. The irony is that most people really know this. And yet, they turn to lawyers anyway. Why is this? Because they really do not understand just why lawyers create the problems that they do, or how they make it more difficult, rather than less difficult, for them to resolve their differences.

It is time that they did. As the following twelve chapters will demonstrate, the idea that turning to the law and to lawyers will help is simply mythology. It is also very dangerous mythology, as can be attested to by the countless numbers of separating and divorcing couples who did so to their regret, and by their children who were invariably caught in the process.

It is time to change this.

Lenard Marlow, J.D.

Huntington, New York
May 1992

THE FIRST MYTH

A Couple's Decision to Separate and Divorce
Leaves Them With a Legal Problem

People rarely consult with lawyers when they get married. Nor do they have a battery of attorneys on hand during their marriage. Nevertheless, at the first thought of separation or divorce, their immediate response is to turn to lawyers and to the law. To make matters worse, they are encouraged by all concerned that this is both a responsible and a necessary thing to do.

Why is this? Why, if a couple was able to resolve the important issues in their lives in the past on their own, without the intervention of lawyers and the law, is it not possible for them to do so now? More to the point, why, if it was neither necessary nor appropriate for them to turn to lawyers and the law before, is it absolutely essential now?

The answer, quite obviously, is that it is not. Common sense is enough to tell us this. If lawyers, who, after all, are simply people who went to law school, did not have some special provence that qualified them to make the decisions in our lives when we were married, they do not now mysteriously acquire this expertise because we have decided to divorce. Similarly, if we would never have considered it appropriate to regulate our personal affairs by the application of abstract legal rules before, those legal principles do not now suddenly become relevant or appropriate simply because we have decided to change the direction of our lives. On the contrary, we have every reason to continue to regulate our lives based upon the same personal considerations that we have always looked to in the past. Again, our common sense is enough to tell us this.

Does this mean that the decisions we made in the past, based on those considerations, were always the best ones? Obviously not. Some of them were and, just as assuredly, some of them probably were not. By the same token, some of the decisions we made were based upon personal considerations with which we mutually agreed, while others had to be hammered out of our different attitudes, individual styles and conflicting points of view. Be that as it may, whatever the result, and whether they were mutually satisfactory or not, one thing is for certain, and that is that lawyers were not invited to participate in our discussions. Nor did we think that it was necessary that they should have been, or feel at a loss because they were not.

What was true in our marriage is equally true in our divorce. If it was sufficient for us to make the important decisions in our lives based upon these personal considerations before, it is no less appropriate for us to do so now. Again, our common sense tells us this. More importantly, our experience confirms it. After all, there are few among us whose personal history does not include the war stories of friends or relatives who, having decided to separate and divorce, turned to lawyers and the law for help, and knowledge of the very heavy price—in terms of time, cost and emotional injury—that they paid in the process. And yet, like lemmings blindly rushing to our fate, at the first thought of divorce, we instinctively draw swords and march off to resolve the problems with which we are confronted by doing legal battle with one another.

Why do we do this? More importantly, if the far more appropriate response is so obvious, why do we not see it? It is because this truth has become lost in a forest of legal mythology. And it is a very thick and deep mythology, as is evidenced by the fact that we cling to it, and are unable to see the simple truth that is hidden by it, in spite of the terrible price that we pay for doing so. If we are ever going to recover this truth, we will have to cut through this thicket of mythology, branch by branch, one at a time.

And what is this simple truth? It is that the fact that we have decided to separate and divorce does not mean that it is no longer possible, let alone appropriate, for us to make the important decisions in our lives as we always have in the past. Rather, it only means that the circumstances that have brought us to this decision make it far more difficult for us to do this. As we will later see, there are some very important implications to this simple truth. However, and before we come to them, it is first necessary to cut through the mythology that prevents us from seeing it.

And so we ask again, why, when we separate and divorce, it is necessary that we turn to lawyers and to the law—that we employ legal procedures—to make the important decisions with which we are faced? It is that our decision to separate and divorce has left us with a legal problem.

This is the first myth of divorce. Our divorce does not leave us with a legal problem. Rather, and as our common sense would tell us if we but stopped to consider it, it leaves us with a *personal* problem—a personal life crisis—that only has only certain legal implications.

Unfortunately, we are so in the habit of viewing divorce as a *legal* problem, requiring a legal solution, that we have long since forgotten this, as self-evident as it is. It will therefore be necessary for us to consider other personal decisions that married couples have been called upon to make in their lives that, like the decision to divorce, have also had legal implications, if we are going to be able to see this.

Let us consider, then, a much earlier decision that a couple who is now divorcing was required to make—we will call them Barbara and Bill. Let us consider their decision to marry. As with their divorce, that decision also had certain legal implications. A license permitting the marriage had to be obtained. There may also have been certain other legal requirements, in terms of blood tests or waiting periods, that had to be compiled with. And, of course, the marriage had to be solemnized in the manner prescribed by the law. But that did not mean that Barbara's and Bill's decision to marry was a legal one, or that they felt that it left them with a legal problem. And lawyers were certainly not called in to give their opinions about, let alone to determine, where Barbara's and Bill's wedding reception should be held, whom they should invite, what they should serve or where they should vacation following its conclusion. Rather, Barbara and Bill considered these to be personal decisions that they, and they alone, were best qualified to make.

Nor were they necessarily of one mind concerning these decisions. On the contrary, there may very well have been substantial differences of opinion between them— Barbara may have wanted a large, formal wedding while Bill would have much preferred a small, more informal one. Perhaps the issue was decided by Bill deferring to Barbara here, on the basis that weddings have a significance to women that they do not have to men. Or they may have worked out a relatively easy accommodation between their differing attitudes and desires. It is even possible that those differences caused a great deal of friction in their relationship and that the issues were resolved only after some difficulty. Regardless of how those decision were ultimately made, however, there is one thing that Barbara and Bill did not do. They did not turn to lawyers to help them make them.

The same was true when they purchased their first home. To be sure, their decision to buy a home had legal implications, as contracts had to be prepared and deeds had to filed. But that did not mean that Barbara and Bill thought that their decision to buy a home left them with a legal problem. And lawyers were not called in to decide in what community they should look, how much they should spend, or whether that home should be a ranch, a colonial or a split level. Rather, they considered these to be personal decisions that they, and they alone, were best qualified to make, on whatever basis was ultimately acceptable to them.

Again, that decision may also have been the occasion for some disagreement between them. One of them may have wanted to buy a home, and the other not to buy a home. They may have been of like mind in their decision to buy a home, but may nevertheless have disagreed as to whether it should have been a new home or a resale, in the country or close to the city. But that did not mean that Barbara and Bill considered these problems to be legal ones, or that they sought legal advice to resolve them. On the contrary, they knew that these were decisions that they, and only they, should make, and that there was no one more qualified to make them.

This distinction between our personal decisions and the legal implications that they have is not very hard to understand. Nor is it something that we have to be taught. On the contrary, we know it almost instinctively. Nevertheless, at the first thought of divorce, all of this changes. It is as if we forget all that we know, and that our best instincts fly out the window. Though it was never true before, we are now absolutely convinced that we have a legal problem.

Why is this? If Barbara and Bill had never felt that their personal decisions left them with legal problems before, why do they think this now? The answer is somewhat complex and a function of the fact that there is an important difference between the decisions that Barbara and Bill were faced with in the past and those that they are called upon to make at the present time. In a very important sense, the decisions that Barbara and Bill had to make in the past were *empowering* decisions. While Barbara and Bill may well have had different opinions concerning them, there was, nevertheless, a commonality in their relationship that tended to promote agreement and help them find the necessary solutions. Thus, Barbara and Bill may well have disagreed as to whether they should have had a large or a small wedding, but they were united in their decision to marry. Even if they were not always united in a particular decision—Barbara wanted to buy a home in the country while Bill wanted to remain in their apartment in the city— they were still united in their common desire to maintain their ongoing relationship (their marriage), and that served to save the day, even if one or both of them was required to make substantial compromises or sacrifices in the process.

Their decision to divorce, however, is not such an em- powering decision. On the contrary, it is a *dis-empowering* one. To begin with, and in the overwhelming majority of instances, it is not a joint decision, at least initially. Thus, while Barbara and Bill each wanted to go in the same gen- eral direction when they married, that is probably not the case now. Rather, and while they each may be unhappy in the marriage, they may still wish to go in very different directions—Bill to end it and Barbara to try to save it. Even if they are of the same mind, however, there will still be a problem, as they have very different, and conflicting, atti- tudes as to why it is and how it is they have come to this point in their lives. And, as we will see later, these differ- ences have given birth to very strong and painful feelings that tend to overwhelm them and make any communication between them difficult, if not impossible.

There is another important difference between the deci- sions with which Barbara and Bill found themselves con- fronted in the past and the decisions with which they are faced now. Up until this point, there was a continuity in their life together, and the decisions that they were required to make took place within the context of an ongoing rela- tionship. That relationship provided certain guidelines and signposts that tended to give direction to their lives, thereby enabling them to make the necessary decisions that were required. Just as importantly, it imposed certain con- straints that not only tended to place limits on how far each of them could go but that also made it necessary for one or both of them to make some accommodations. Now, however, and with one swift blow, that relationship has come to an end and, with it, the security and common direction that it previously provided. As a result, Barbara and Bill now find themselves being pulled in opposite directions. Worse yet, one or both of them may well feel that they are absolutely lost and adrift at sea, and not know in which direction to turn. To add to their dilemma, the terrible feelings that so overwhelm one or both of them make it difficult, and sometimes impossible, for the two of them to sit down, in common cause, and address the problems with which they are faced. In fact, in most cases like Barbara's and Bill's, there is not even enough trust left for them to try.

It is at this point that legal mythology steps in to persuade Barbara and Bill that what they have is a legal problem. They have a legal problem because it is only by looking to the law that they will be able to get their bearings and determine just where they are and what they should do. Worse yet, that legal mythology persuades them that it is only by employing separate lawyers that they will each be able to navigate themselves through these troubled waters. Moreover, they are encouraged in this strange belief by all concerned—even by those who, through their own personal experience, should know better.

By what artful sleight of hand does legal mythology accomplish this? Quite simply, by causing Barbara and Bill to confuse the problem they have—the fact that their decision to divorce has left them with certain questions that the two of them must resolve—with the legal procedures that they have been persuaded to employ in an effort to resolve them. In short, Barbara and Bill have a legal problem only because they have taken their personal problem and made it into one.

Let us illustrate this. Suppose that Barbara and Bill had been able to resolve all of the issues they were faced with on their own. As was the case when they married and when they bought their home, they sat down together and decided who would have custody of their children and where their children would live. They also determined the amount that would be paid for their support and who would pay their unreimbursed medical expenses. They even decided on the division of their property and who would be responsible for their outstanding debts. In fact, they were able to resolve all of the questions that had been raised by their decision to separate and divorce.

Would we still say that Barbara's and Bill's decision to separate and divorce had left them with a legal problem? More importantly, would it make any sense to do this? To be sure, there are certain legal implications in their decision—agreements have to be drawn and signed, and papers have to be filed with the court. But these are by and large ministerial legal acts, not the kinds of things that we talk about when we say of someone that he or she has a legal problem.

If it is not the fact that Barbara and Bill have decided to separate and divorce that causes them to have a legal problem, and if it is not even the fact that their decision has left them with important questions that they must resolve, what then does? As we have said, it is only the fact that they have turned to lawyers and to the law to help them resolve these problems. Was it necessary for Barbara and Bill to do this? More importantly, would they have made a mistake, or broken any law, if they had not? The question, quite obviously, is a rhetorical one. The fact that the two of them could have worked out all of these problems on their own is proof of that.

Suppose, however, that Barbara and Bill were not able to resolve these issues on their own. Suppose, in fact, that they were at loggerheads with respect to most of them. Did that necessarily mean that they then had a legal problem or that they had to turn to the law? After all, there are a hundred and one other procedures people could employ to resolve a problem or settle a dispute. They could flip a coin, and if the issue was who was to get the newer of two television sets, that might be a perfectly appropriate procedure to employ if they could not work it out on some other basis—certainly far better than going off and doing legal battle with one another. They might seek the good offices and opinion of a friend or relative to help them resolve it. Or, and as silly as it may seem—though, as we will see, not as silly as it may at first blush appear—they could even determine it by playing a game of chess. Suppose that they decide to resolve the dispute by playing a game of chess. Would we now say that they had a chess problem? More to the point, would it make any sense for us to do this?

If Barbara and Bill find themselves with a legal problem, therefore, it is only because they have chosen to resolve the questions at issue by turning to the law and to legal procedures. To put it another way, Barbara and Bill have a legal problem only because they have decided to resolve it by playing a game of legal chess. Unfortunately, separating and divorcing couples have been doing this for so long that Barbara and Bill can no longer see this. Worse yet, and since they will be encouraged by all concerned that this is not only necessary, but also a sane and sensible thing to do, it would never occur to them that it might be otherwise.

Since legal myths do not exist in a vacuum—since we see the emperor's new clothes only because all of those around us insist that he is wearing them—it is perhaps appropriate to pause for a moment and identify those who give support to this legal mythology and who, often unwittingly, will cause Barbara and Bill to accept it blindly, and as if it were gospel. It is particularly appropriate since those involved do not do Barbara and Bill any favor. On the contrary, all that they do is send them off down a blind alley from which, all too often, there is no return.

Whenever a couple decides to separate and divorce, and particularly when they make that fact known publicly, there tends to arise around each of them a group of people—a group whom we call the Greek Chorus of well-wishers.

These are the people who, from the sidelines, offer them aid and encouragement, provide them with information, give them moral support and urge them on. They include not only friends and relatives, but therapists, clergymen and lawyers, as well. In fact, they include anyone who comments on, or makes judgments about, what is taking place.

Will the advice that Barbara and Bill receive from their respective Greek Choruses be to sit down, as they have always done in the past, and, putting aside the difficult feelings with which they are struggling, attempt to resolve these matters on their own? Even if they do not recommend this, will it be to urge them to consider some other sane, sensible procedure to address the problems with which they are faced? The answer, unfortunately, is no. On the contrary, and accepting the mythology that their divorce has left them with a legal problem, Barbara's and Bill's Greek Choruses will summarily, and unthinkingly, send them off to lawyers. Worse yet, and to a man, they will do this convinced that they have served them well with the advice that they have given them.

Unfortunately, and as Barbara and Bill will learn all too late, they have not. For in reinforcing the mythology that their divorce has left them with a legal problem, and in thereby making it one, all that the Greek Chorus of well-wishers will have done will be to send Barbara and Bill off into lawyer-land and to commit them to legal warfare.

Couples who make the error of confusing the *problems* associated with their divorce with the *procedures* that have traditionally been employed to resolve them pay a very heavy price for their mistake. Unfortunately, as Bill and Barbara will learn, their children will pay an even heavier price.

THE SECOND MYTH

What Is at Issue
In a Couple's Separation and Divorce
Is the Determination
Of Their Legal Rights and Obligations

In the past, when Barbara and Bill found themselves faced with a personal problem, they employed a very simple procedure. They sat down—perhaps around their kitchen table—and worked it out on their own. Nor would it have occurred to them to do anything else. After all, it was their problem, and who had a better right, or was more qualified, to do so.

Once they decide to separate and divorce, however, all of this changes. As we have seen, legal mythology, and the Greek Chorus that acts as its messenger, insists that a couple's decision to divorce has presented them with a legal problem and that it is therefore no longer appropriate for them to resolve the important issues in their lives as they have done in the past. It may have been appropriate for them to have decided these questions on their own while they were married. However, now that they are divorcing, it is essential that lawyers be there to participate in their discussions. In fact, it is essential that these discussions be conducted by lawyers.

Legal mythology has done more, however, than to persuade Barbara and Bill that they must employ a very different procedure—that they must substitute a lawyer's conference room or a courtroom in place of their own kitchen table. It has also persuaded them that they must judge the decisions they make by a very different yardstick. Until now, they had made the decisions in their lives based upon nothing other than personal considerations—upon the factors they considered to be important. Nor would it have occurred to them to do otherwise. After all, these were their decisions, not others'. If that were so, why would they have based them on any other considerations or judged them by any other yardstick?

Now that they have decided to divorce, however, they have been persuaded—generally without consciously being aware of it—that these considerations and this yardstick are no longer appropriate. Since their divorce has left them with a legal problem, it is not only necessary that they employ legal procedures. It is also necessary that they measure whatever decisions they come to against legal yardsticks.

Let us illustrate this. Last spring, Barbara and Bill were faced with the question of what arrangements they would make that coming summer for their youngest son, John, who was then ten years of age. In particular, the issue was whether they should send him to day camp. In making that decision, they asked themselves a number of questions. Could they afford to send him to day camp? If they could not afford to send him for the entire summer, would they be able to send him for half of it? What kind of activities did the day camp provide and was the supervision adequate? Was it an experience that John would enjoy and perhaps even benefit from? Since both parents worked and had to make arrangements for their son over the summer, what other alternatives were available? Based upon these and a number of other considerations, Barbara and Bill finally decided to send John to day camp for four weeks, to take him on a trip up the coast for two weeks during their own vacation and to have him spend the balance of the summer with Barbara's parents, who owned a home in the mountains.

This past winter, Bill and Barbara separated. A few months later, they again found themselves faced with the question of whether they would send John to day camp that summer, a question that was now all the more complicated by the fact that John had very much enjoyed camp the previous summer and was anxious to return. Unfortunately, when the question came up, an issue arose as to who would pay for it. Barbara insisted that Bill should pay for day camp because he earned significantly more money than she did. Bill, on the other hand, felt that Barbara should pay for at least a portion of it. Unable to resolve the problem with Barbara, and persuaded that he and Barbara now had a legal problem, Bill decided to discuss the matter with an attorney.

Did Bill's attorney raise any of the questions, or invoke any of the considerations, that he and Barbara had previously discussed, when they were confronted with this same issue the year before? The answer, of course, is no. After all, what could he possibly have added that would have been of any significance? He was not a financial planner. Nor was he a child psychologist, let alone an authority on what was in John's best interests. In fact, he had no special provence that would have qualified him to participate in those discussions during their marriage. If that was the case, what would suddenly make him an expert in these matters now, simply because they had decided to get a divorce?

There is another reason why Bill's attorney did not raise any of these questions. These may well have been the criteria that Barbara and Bill employed in making the personal decisions in their lives while they were married. But they are not the criteria that lawyers employ once a couple decides to divorce. The question that Bill's attorney asked, therefore, was a very different one. It was: Did Bill have a legal obligation to send John to day camp?

Did Bill's attorney's question really make any sense? More to the point, was it more appropriate than the questions

Barbara and Bill had asked each other when they were confronted with this same issue the year before? And if it really was such an important question, why had Bill and Barbara not asked themselves that question then? It makes no difference. Legal rules are a lawyer's stock in trade. In fact, they are all that a lawyer really knows. And so, that is the yardstick Bill's lawyer will employ to determine what Bill, who is now his client, should do. Worse yet, he will subtly and, as we will later see, not so subtly, persuade Bill that not only is this legal yardstick the correct measuring stick to apply, but that he might make a mistake, and would be a fool in the bargain, were he to apply any other.

How is it that we have come to substitute legal rules for the personal considerations that we have always employed in the past? More importantly, why have we allowed ourselves to be persuaded that it makes any sense to do this? After all, there is really nothing very special about legal rules. In fact, they are based on very abstract principles that have little, if anything, to do with the reality of our individual lives. If we had never thought to employ them before, why is it that we must do so now? And why do we think that we would be making a mistake if we did not?

The answer that we will be given by our Greek Chorus is twofold. First, we employ legal rules because, as the experience of so many separating and divorcing couples demonstrates, we are no longer able to make these decisions on our own, based upon the personal considerations that we employed in the past. If proof of this is needed, it will be found in the fact that we are required to turn to lawyers and to the law to resolve them. Second, and more important, we turn to the law and to legal rules because it is no longer appropriate that we base the important decisions in our lives—certainly not those associated with our divorce—on nothing more substantial than personal considerations. These considerations may have been sufficient when we were married, and when the decisions we were called upon to make were for both of us. Now we are divorcing, however, and that means that we must think of ourselves.

Since separating and divorcing couples pay a very heavy price in summarily accepting these answers, it is appropriate that we stop to consider them and to ask ourselves whether they really have any merit. For, in truth, they do not. The idea that it is either appropriate or necessary to conduct our affairs, or to make the important decisions in our lives, on the basis of legal rules is not the better part of wisdom. It is legal nonsense. And if separating and divorcing couples accept this nonsense it is not because it appeals to their reason or even to their common sense. It is because they have allowed the fear and anger, and the hundred and one other emotions that so overwhelm them, to cloud their better judgment.

Contrary to legal mythology, a couple's divorce does not mean that it is no longer possible for them to resolve the important issues in their lives as they have in the past. It means only that it will be more difficult—perhaps even far more difficult—for them to do this. But that does not mean that they should not try. Nor does it excuse our summarily suggesting some other procedure—let alone one as irresponsible as sending them off to do legal battle with one another—as a substitute for such effort. After all, these personal considerations are no less important now than they were before simply because a couple has decided to separate and divorce. More importantly, legal rules, which they had never thought to employ before, do not suddenly become more relevant on that account. They are still only abstract principles that have little, if anything, to do with the realities of our individual lives.

The answer, therefore, is not to put those personal considerations aside. Nor is it to rush off and substitute other criteria in their place. Rather, and as more and more separating and divorcing couples are learning, it is to find a way to resolve the issues with which they are confronted, based upon those personal considerations that are important to them, despite the fact that their decision to divorce has made that more difficult.

Divorce lawyers' objection that now that we are divorcing we must think of ourselves is also wanting. Worse yet, it is simply verbal sleight of hand. We are always thinking of ourselves—it is impossible not to. And this is as true in our marriage as it is in our divorce. Marrying someone, after all, is not an act of charity, any more than divorcing that same person is an act of spite. In both instances, we are making a judgment in terms of what we believe to be our best interests. This, after all, is what it means to make a decision based upon personal considerations.

To be sure, and since we make the decisions in our lives within the context of the relationships that we have with others, these decisions will necessarily be affected by the fact that these people are important to us. They may also be affected by the fact that it is often necessary to balance our own needs against the legitimate needs of the other people who inhabit the world in which we live and with whom we do business. And, to be sure, we will also balance these decisions in terms of our own personal sense of what is right and wrong. But the balancing that takes place, and the adjustment that we make based upon our own needs and these other factors, is still ultimately based upon those personal considerations that are important to us. Nor could it be otherwise.

Invoking the idea that, because we are separating and divorcing, we must now think of ourselves, is thus no answer. It is simply to ignore the question. For while our individual decisions are now affected by different personal considerations than they previously were, these decisions are still affected by considerations that are personal to us. Moreover, and while it is still appropriate that we make the decisions in our lives based upon personal considerations, if we are able to do that, it is also just as appropriate that we balance these against those other considerations that have always guided our decisions in the past.

Consider the previous example. It may well be that Bill was willing to make certain personal sacrifices in order to send John to camp during the period in which he and Barbara were married that he is not willing to make now. It may even be that there are certain factors, derivative of his and Barbara's decision to divorce, that cause him to look at the whole problem very differently. And, to be sure, it is even possible that certain of his feelings, which are a by-product of the considerations that have brought him and Barbara to this point in their lives, are prejudicing his thinking and clouding the issue. But these, nevertheless, are still the factors—the personal considerations—that are important to Bill. And these are still the considerations that he should be helped to sort out and adjust in order that he and Barbara may come to an appropriate resolution of the issues with which they are confronted. To be sure, their divorce may make this much more difficult. But it does not change the problem.

There is another difficulty with this answer, and it is that it assumes that just as the parties are of two minds now, because they are divorcing, that they were necessarily always of one mind before, because they were married. Nothing could be farther from the truth. Married couples are not always of one mind. If they were, how do we explain the fact that they are now divorcing. Similarly, divorcing couples are not necessarily of two minds about everything. They have different opinions only about some things. Thus, their decision to divorce does not pose a problem for them that they never had before. It just poses that problem in a different way.

The answer is wanting for yet another reason. It may well be that a couple's decision to divorce is a more significant change than any that has taken place in their relationship before. But it is not the only change. In fact, there were probably many other changes that took place during their marriage that also significantly affected the personal considerations that one or both of them deemed to be important. Moreover, each of those changes required that the couple effectuate an appropriate balance between those conflicting considerations that were personal to each of them. Their decision to divorce, therefore, does not present them with a different problem. As we have said, it only presents them with a more difficult one. Thus, while, in the past, the couple was able to mediate those conflicting personal considerations on their own, they are now going to need some help.

There is one final difficulty with the idea that, because we are divorcing, we must now think of ourselves. The issue is not whether we should be thinking of ourselves, now that we have decided to divorce. Of course we should. It is whether the decisions that will be made incident to our divorce will be acceptable only to ourselves—only to one of us—rather than to both of us. Clearly, there can be no question as to which of these choices is preferable. The decisions that a couple will have to make are not simply words that will be written on a piece of paper. They are commitments that will have to be carried out, usually over a long period of time. Nor are they self-enforcing. That being the case, it makes far more sense for them to conclude an agreement that they both feel they can live with, rather than an agreement that is acceptable only to one of them. And all of the talk that, now that they are divorcing, they must think only of themselves will not change that.

Let us carry the argument one step further, however. Let us assume that a couple's decision to separate and divorce does, in fact, make it impossible for them to resolve the issues with which they are confronted in the same manner, and based upon the same kinds of personal considerations, that they have always employed in the past. Let us even assume, again for the sake of argument, that it would not be appropriate for them to do this, even if they could.

This still leaves us with a question. Why should they employ legal rules to resolve these issues? After all, and as we noted previously, there are any one of a number of procedures that they can employ for this purpose. They can flip a coin. They can have a foot race. Or they can play a game of chess. Why is it better for them to resolve these issues by the application of legal rules—in other words, to play a game of legal chess—rather than to employ any of these other procedures? Certainly these other procedures are quicker and far less expensive. And, as we will later see, they are also far more decisive. If resolving these issues by the application of legal rules is to be justified, therefore, some other basis will have to be found.

This brings us to the second myth of divorce. It is one thing to say that it is no longer possible or appropriate for separating and divorcing couples to resolve the important issues in their lives as they have done before, or to judge these issues on the basis of the personal considerations that they have always employed. It is quite another, as we will see, to justify their substituting arbitrary legal rules, having little to do with the realities of their individual lives. How, then, do lawyers persuade them to do this? They do it by another feat of legal sleight of hand. Lawyers do not refer to legal rules as being arbitrary principles having little, if anything, to do with the realities of our individual lives. Instead, they refer to them, and thereby sanctify their use, by calling them legal rights.

Labels, of course, do not change reality. If I refer to the pencil with which I write as being a right-handed, semi-automatic, graphite-filled writing instrument, equipped with an erasing component, I may have made it sound more impressive. But it is still only a pencil. The same, of course, is true of legal rules. All the fancy talk aside, they are still only the rules we apply when we can't find better ones. Unfortunately, referring to them not as legal rules but as legal rights causes us to lose sight of this.

We have done more than that, however. With the same stroke, we have also disqualified all others. For in characterizing legal rules as legal rights, we have made them into legal entitlements—the definition of what is rightfully ours, and what we justly deserve. In short, legal rules have become the expression of our God-given rights—rights that, if they do not flow from Mt. Sinai, at the very least emanate from the United States Constitution. If these legal rules were only just a better set of considerations than the personal considerations that we had always employed in the past, it might make sense for us to employ them. But it wouldn't be necessary. And we would certainly not be breaking any law if we didn't. By referring to legal rules as legal rights, however, all of this changes. To employ any other considerations would be to deny us what is rightfully ours and what we are justly due. To employ any other yardstick—even the personal considerations that we employed in the past—would be to run the risk that we might get it wrong.

There are some very unfortunate consequences to this. No longer being able to see legal rules as simply the rules we apply when we can't find better ones, the determination of these rules, now called legal rights, quickly becomes the primary objective. Whereas these rules were originally important only as a means of resolving the issues that Barbara and Bill were unable to resolve on their own, their determination has now become an end in itself. To use an analogy that we invoked previously, it is as if, having decided to resolve their dispute by playing a game of chess, and convinced that they now had a chess problem, Barbara and Bill felt compelled to run out and buy books on chess to find out what their respective chess rights were—how the game is played, the strategies that should be employed and how they are allowed to move their attacking and defending armies across the board. Realizing the limits of their own knowledge and skill, however, they also felt compelled to go out and hire chess champions to advise them and to direct the play. In time, and since their respective champions are the experts, their champions completely take over the play. In fact, neither Barbara nor Bill would make a move without their respective champions. For, were they to do this, they would run the risk of losing the game. And winning, of course, is what the game is all about.

As we have noted, this has some very unfortunate consequences. The worst of these is that Barbara and Bill have made the proper determination of these rules, now called rights, more important than the problem that they were invoked to solve. In fact—and this is something to which we will return later—they have made their proper determination so important that the resolution of their dispute has become but a secondary consideration. At times, it appears as if the resolution of their differences is not important at all. Rights, after all, are very important. We have been brought up to view them as being inalienably ours, and the things that make life worth living. In fact, they are so important that we believe that at times they are even worth fighting for and dying for. That being the case, they are not, like the personal considerations we have always employed in the past, something that we see as being compromisable, or as subordinate to other, more practical, considerations. Thus, we often justify them, and the very incredible lengths that we go to defend them, by saying that they represent questions of principle.

The problem does not reside simply with the fact that we have come to see see legal rules as being legal rights. It also stems from our failure to distinguish between two different kinds of legal rights. While it may make sense to talk about the guarantees provided by the first ten amendments to the United States Constitution as representing rights, and even inalienable rights, that we have, it does not make the same sense to say that because the legislature has enacted a law making the speed limit fifty-five miles an hour, that one of our rights is to drive our automobiles at fifty-five miles an hour. We have that right only because the legislature has enacted a law making that a permissible speed at which to drive. Thus, should the legislature later lower that speed limit to fifty miles an hour, we might question its collective judgment. We might even try to get the legislature to reconsider its decision. But we would not complain that an important right of ours had been abridged. These are simply the rules of the road. We have had different rules in the past, and we will undoubtedly have different rules in the future. These are simply the rules that we happen to have today.

Although it is not generally appreciated, the same is true of the rules that are applied by courts to the resolution of disputes between husbands and wives incident to their divorce. Suppose, for instance, that the law provided that alimony was to be awarded on a permanent basis—that if Barbara were entitled to receive alimony, she would be entitled to receive it until she remarried or until either she or Bill died. If that were the case, it would certainly make sense to say that Barbara had the right to apply to a court for permanent support. But that does not mean that her right to permanent alimony is one of her legal rights, as we normally use that term. After all, if the legislature were to amend the divorce law to provide that permanent alimony would be awarded only in marriages of long duration, and where the recipient wife were more than fifty-five years of age, or were they to eliminate permanent alimony altogether, Barbara's rights would not have been violated in the process. All that it would mean would be that the rules of the road had been changed again, as they had been so many times in the past.

The second error in viewing legal rules as legal rights is a natural consequence of the first. If we saw that what a separating and divorcing couple was faced with was fundamentally a personal problem, then almost any procedure Bill and Barbara might employ to resolve it would do. As we said, if the issue was who was to get the newer of two television sets, they could even settle it by flipping a coin. By elevating legal rules to legal rights, however, the effect has been to disqualify all procedures but one—even all of the other procedures that Barbara and Bill might employ that made far more sense. Incredibly, the elevation of legal rules to legal rights has even disqualified the one method they have always employed in the past, namely, to sit down and work out the problem on their own. Worse yet, they have been left with the feeling that, if they were to sit down and try to work out their problems, they might make a mistake and get it wrong.

Legal mythology aside, Barbara and Bill have two, and only two, rights. One is the right to sit down and attempt to resolve the important issues that their divorce has confronted them with, based upon the personal considerations that they have always employed. The other right is to run off and do legal battle with one another, resolving those same issues with the application of a set of substantive and procedural rules that have no more relevance to their lives today than they did before. It will not do to obfuscate this obvious fact by referring to these rules as rights. Nor will it do to give priority to this procedure, and to disqualify all others, by suggesting that it is the only one which will vouchsafe those rights.

There is another point that must be made. Sanctifying the rules that courts apply to resolve disputes between divorcing couples, by referring to them as legal rights, belies another important difference that exists between the kinds of rights that people have. Let us illustrate this. If Barbara had received notification that she had won the lottery, it would obviously make sense to say that she had a right to the prize that went to the winner. However, to say that she also has the right to have her dispute with Bill resolved by the application of the rules that courts apply, and that she believes will be of benefit to her, is not the same kind of right. After all, if she has the right to resort to legal proceedings and to a court of law for that purpose, Bill also has the right to fight her every step of the way. It may be unfair, and perhaps even irresponsible, for him to do this. It may even prove ultimately pointless. Nevertheless, and as with Barbara, it is his absolute right.

It is important that Barbara remember this. In fact, in the adversarial world in which these rules are applied, it is simply not possible for her to forget it. Legal mythology notwithstanding, legal rights do not exist in a vacuum. Nor are they there simply for the asking. Rather, they are the end point of a legal process. But since that process is an adversarial one, Barbara will have to fight to get them. Nor does the fact that she is entitled to them—that they represent her legal rights—change that.

There is something else that it would be well for Barbara to remember. Wars are not always won by those who are virtuous, or even by those who have right on their side. More often than not, wars are won by those who are the strongest and most persistent. They are also sometimes won by those who play foul rather than fair. It is wonderful to say that Barbara has the right to apply to a court for permanent support. But suppose Bill wears her down, and delays the proceedings to the point that she is compelled to give up and give in before she gets there. As we have said, it may not be nice for him to do this. Nevertheless, in the adversarial world in which legal rules are applied, this is his right also.

The relationship between legal rules and the setting in which those rules are applied is a theme that we will have occasion to return to at a later point, as it has implications far more significant than has generally been appreciated. For the time being, however, it is enough to remind ourselves where we began. It is the *problems* with which separating and divorcing couples find themselves confronted that is the issue, not the *procedures* that they employ to resolve those problems. Sanctifying those procedures, as the law has done, does not solve their problem. All that it does is to make them lose sight of it.

THE THIRD MYTH

If Separating and Divorcing Couples Do Not Look
To the Law and to Legal Rules
They Run the Risk of Making a Mistake
And Getting It Wrong

As we have seen, there are any one of a number of procedures that separating and divorcing couples could employ
to resolve their differences. The simplest, of course, would
be to flip a coin. But, and understandably so, they do not
want the important matters in their lives left to chance.
They could settle their differences by means of a contest.
Nor, however, do they want them resolved by a question of
strength or endurance. They could even leave their determination to the outcome of a game of chess. But they are not
even willing to substitute skill as the appropriate arbiter.

Nor would there be many amongst us who would quar-
rel with this, or suggest otherwise. After all, as enlightened
people, we have long since discarded trial by combat and
trial by ordeal. For similar reasons, we have also outlawed
dueling as an appropriate means to resolve questions of
honor and principle, even though it was once considered to
be not only appropriate, but absolutely necessary. Rather,
we want the important questions in our lives to be resolved
more sensibly and on the basis of more rational considerations.

This leaves us with a problem. For if we would not
accept any of those procedures, why then would we accept
a contest between lawyers, playing a game of legal chess—

legal gladiators engaged in legal combat? The answer is because we believe that there is something special about the legal rules that will govern their play. We have been brought up to identify the law with justice, and the legal procedures employed by courts as the vehicle whereby that justice will be achieved. Legal rules may not represent our inalienable rights. And it may be that we have never employed them to resolve the important issues in our lives before. But they are still more than simply the rules of the road. They represent society's considered opinion as to what is appropriate. They represent what is just and fair. In short, they are not the rules that we apply when we can't find better ones. They are the better ones.

This is the third myth of divorce. Nevertheless, and as with the other mythology that fuels adversarial legal proceedings, separating and divorcing couples summarily accept it, despite the very heavy price that they will have to pay in doing so. For what, after all, has been the effect of sanctifying legal rules and elevating them to a place of special status? Is it to have given us answers and thereby solved our problems? As we will later see, that, unfortunately, is not the case. All that it has done is convince us that, should we fail to apply them, and attempt, instead, to resolve them by some other means, there is a danger we may make a mistake. It makes no difference that we have never stopped to consider legal rules before, let alone to insist that they be applied to our everyday decisions. Nor does it make any difference that we have just gone about the business of our lives, resolving these issues on our own, unconcerned with whether we got it right. By sanctifying legal rules, legal mythology has intimidated us into believing that, should we ignore them, we may get it wrong.

How is it that we have come to believe that the law, and the judges who apply it, are capable of making the correct decisions in our personal lives, let alone that this is one of their functions? More importantly, why do we believe this now when we would never have accepted it before? Suppose that at the time Bill and Barbara were considering purchasing their first home, they had decided to seek the law's guidance. Knowing that our laws had been carefully thought out, and that they expressed the considered judgment of the ages, they decided to consult with an attorney to aid them in their decision and, in particular, to advise them whether they should purchase a home and, if so, whether it should be a ranch house or a colonial. As we all know, they would have received very little help. In fact, what they would have been told was that, contrary to their assumption, the law did not have any special province here and that, in its wisdom, it concluded that these matters should best be left to the two of them to decide.

When will the law be willing to help us? they had asked. Only if there is some dispute between you that you can't settle by some other means, they were answered. But there is such a dispute, they had advised their attorney: One of us feels that we should stay where we now live, while the other feels that we should move and purchase a new home. Again Barbara and Bill would have gotten very little help from the law. The law, they would have been told, does not provide all of the rules that we should follow in the conduct of our lives. It does not even attempt to decide all of the disputes that we have. Just as importantly, it does not consider its judgment to be superior to our own. And so Barbara and Bill would have gone away frustrated in the belief that it was the function of the law to help them in times such as this, and that it was able to do that.

There are, of course, times when the law will step in to resolve our disputes. One such instance is when those disputes are the result of our decision to separate and divorce. Nevertheless, the fact that the law will step in and apply legal rules to our disputes if they are incident to our separation and divorce does not mean that the law suddenly acquired a wisdom that it previously lacked, let alone that the application of legal rules will now guarantee the correct result that they were unable to guarantee before. And, most importantly, it does not mean that there is now the danger that we may get it wrong if we resolve them on our own, or on some other basis.

Suppose that, having decided to separate and divorce, one of the issues with which Barbara and Bill were again confronted was whether or not they would enroll their son John in day camp over the summer. Suppose, also, that they had been able to sit down and discuss this as they had in the past, and had come to the conclusion that they would send him to camp and that they would split the cost equally between themselves. What sense would it make to suggest to them that, to make sure they hadn't made a mistake and come to the wrong decision, they should check to see what the result would have been had they applied legal rules? It may well have been that, had they not been able to resolve the issue on their own, Bill would have gone off to an attorney to inquire whether or not he had a legal obligation to send John to day camp, rather than to have asked the better and more appropriate question; namely, whether or not it would be a good idea if he did. But that doesn't mean that he would have come away with a better answer. It just means that, applying different criteria (rules), he may have come away with a different one.

Perhaps this is true with the less important issues that Barbara and Bill will be faced with when they separate and divorce. But that does not mean that the same is also true with the more important issues. Certainly as to these, the wisdom that is reflected in our legal rules is the best judge of what is appropriate or inappropriate. Certainly here, Barbara and Bill would be running the risk of making a serious mistake were they to ignore them.

Is this really so? To test this, let us take what has to be the most important issue with which Barbara and Bill will be faced, namely, the well being of their children and whether it will be best served by their being in their mother's custody and care or in the custody and care of their father. Let us suppose, once again, that in disregard of these rules, and without knowledge of them, Barbara and Bill had sat down and decided that their children would maintain their primary residence with Barbara and had agreed upon scheduled periods of time that they would spend with Bill. Should they be concerned that, not having made their decisions based upon the application of legal rules (what is described by the law as being "in the child's best interests"), and, in fact, having made them in total ignorance of them, they may have made a mistake?

The question, quite obviously, is a rhetorical one. The fact that a judge, if called upon to make this determination, will employ a different set of criteria, one that, he will claim, is based upon their child's "best interests," should not be taken literally, and only a fool would do so. To begin with, and absent those very rare instances where the breach of minimal societal standards is involved, it is never in a child's best interests that a decision concerning his well-being be made by a judge rather than by his parents, if they are capable of making that decision themselves. Moreover, just as legal rules are not endowed with any special significance simply because we refer to them as legal rights, a decision made by a judge is not elevated to any special status simply because, in announcing it, he declares that he has made it based upon their child's "best interests."

A judge, after all, has to know what a child's best interests are before he can make a decision based upon those interests. But what qualifies a judge to know this? Surely there is nothing either in his training or in his experience that would give him those qualifications. Nor will the legal rules that he will turn to provide him with that guidance; for they are, at best, a very poor instrument by which to determine those best interests. That is why a judge's declaration that his decision represents what is in a child's best interest is not judicial wisdom, but judicial arrogance. A judge makes this decision, not because he is qualified to, but because he has to—because Barbara and Bill, in being unable to decide it themselves, have left him with no choice.

In truth, we really know this. And yet we still buy legal mythology and cling to the belief that the legal rules judges invoke, and the procedures lawyers employ to apply them, will somehow guarantee that justice will be done. Why do we do this? We do it out of fear. The prospects of a separation and divorce are very frightening, particularly when it comes to money. As a result, we are afraid that we may get it wrong, and that we may therefore not have enough. Since the law provides rules to decide such questions, and since Barbara and Bill see those rules as representing what is fair and just, it is to the law, therefore, that they turn for guidance. Moreover, they unthinkingly assume that the answers they will be given by the law, and by the application of legal rules, are the right ones.

It will be easy enough to dispel this mythology, however. For if legal rules do embody the wisdom of the ages and guarantee some necessary justice—if they will in fact provide us with the right answers—then they should satisfy some very simple requirements. The first of these is that they should produce results that are just, rather than results that insult our intelligence or seem to us to be clearly unjust.

To test this, we will consider another set of rules that are applied by the law to decide what a husband or wife should receive from the other upon the termination of their marriage. However, in this instance, we will look to the rules that are applied by the law not when marriages are terminated by divorce but when they are terminated by death. There are a number of reasons for choosing this set of rules. First, it is fair to assume that marriages that are terminated by death were more successful than marriages that were terminated by divorce, and that the law should therefore be more generous to the surviving spouse. Second, since fault or misconduct was not a precipitating cause, those considerations should not cloud the issue, and the law's answer should therefore make more sense and be more just. Finally, since the same emotions do not attach to death as to divorce, we should be able to look at the situation more objectively.

What right, then, will a wife have to share in her husband's estate upon his death? The answer generally depends upon the number of children that her husband has at the time of his death. Thus, in the state of New York, a wife is entitled to receive one half of his estate if he has no children, or if he has only one child who is alive at the time of his death. On the other hand, if he has two or more children who are alive at his death, then his wife is only entitled to receive one third of his estate. The rule is very simple, and its application, therefore, is just as simple. There is only one problem, and that is that its application can result in tremendous inequities. Why is this? It is because the number of children that a wife's husband has is considered by the law to be the only relevant circumstance.

Thus, a wife in a childless marriage of but one year will be entitled to receive a greater percentage of her husband's estate than will a wife who has been married to her husband for thirty years and has borne him four children. Similarly, in neither instance will the amount that the wife will receive be dependent upon the contribution that she made to the marriage, or upon how devoted she was to her husband. All wives are entitled to the same percentage of their husbands' estates, whether they were the best of wives or the worst of wives, whether they be old and infirm or young and healthy. Does this make any sense? More importantly, will there be any among us who will be convinced that this represents what is fair and just? It makes no difference. These are the rules and these, therefore, are their legal rights.

To be sure, the equitable distribution laws enacted by the various states in the 1970s and 1980s—those that declared that marriage was now to be considered a total partnership, an economic as well as an emotional one—

represent an attempt to effectuate a more equitable distribution of the property that was acquired during a couple's
marriage. Nevertheless, the fact that the law announces
that its purpose is to do what is fair and equitable does not
mean than equity will be done. And it certainly does not
mean that the law will be successful in convincing Barbara
or Bill that such has been the case. In fact, the experience
of the vast majority of separating and divorcing couples
who turn to the law is just the opposite.

Why is this? Because in making the judgments that it
does, the law is simply incapable of considering all of the
factors, let alone the subtleties and nuances, that make up
the fabric of our individual lives. As a result, it deals in
more-general, all-inclusive principles. For the same reason,
it tends to deal more with concrete realities than with intan-
gibles. In doing this, however, it often ignores just those
factors that are most significant to us and that most affect
what we consider to be appropriate or inappropriate, fair
or unfair. This is why we say that legal rules, particularly
as they are applied to the resolution of our personal disputes, often appear to be very arbitrary, having little, if
anything, to do with the realities of our individual lives.
And this is why Barbara and Bill will more often than not
come away from the court's decision feeling that an injustice has been done.

There is a second problem with the idea that legal rules
are a necessary guarantor of justice. In the previous example that we gave dealing with a wife's right to a portion of
her husband's estate upon his death, we would probably
have been of one mind that the application of legal rules
did not do justice. That being the case, the solution is very
simple. All that we have to do is change those rules. Unfortunately, that will not be as easy as it may at first appear.
For while we may all claim that what we want is a result
that is fair and just, that does not mean that we will agree
on what it looks like. Rather, and like beauty, we will find
that it is more in the eye of the beholder. Thus, though we

may all agree that this rule of law is not fair, and leads to a result that is unjust, that does not mean that we will agree on what a fair and just result would be. Rather, and like Barbara and Bill, we will probably not be of one mind here.

This brings us to yet another problem with the mythology that legal rules embody some special wisdom or guarantee that justice will be done. Legal rules, after all, were not handed down etched in stone tablets. Nor do they represent the expression of eternal principles or, for that matter, the even flow of reasoned judgment. Rather, they are the ever changing rules that were forged in the political process from which they were born. In broad terms, they may well represent, as Justice Oliver Wendell Holmes suggested, society's response to the felt necessities of the times. Nevertheless, in large measure they constitute the compromises that were hammered out between the various constituencies that represent society, and the competing interests and points of view they reflect. That is why, like politics itself, legal rules are a reflection, not of what is right, but of what was possible.

The fact that legal rules represent what was possible rather than what is right does violence, of course, to the idea that they are the instrument that will guarantee that justice will be done. Nevertheless, our modern divorce laws (the equitable distribution statutes enacted by the various states for the very purpose of attempting to do justice between husbands and wives at the time of their divorce) were born of just such a process, and therefore bear that mark. And, as we will see, it is a mark that undermines our rather naive belief that the law and justice are synonymous.

Let us consider this. If legal rules do, in fact, guarantee that justice will be done—that the ultimate agreement concluded between the parties will be fair—then we would expect that they would express principles so clear, and so universally true, that those legal rules would be the same everywhere. Unfortunately, they are not. On the contrary, they vary considerably. Thus, while a wife in the state of

Oregon or Massachusetts may be told that it is her legal right to receive support from her husband following their divorce, since the court in Texas has no power to direct a husband to pay support to his wife, the same wife in the state of Texas will be told that she has no such right. While a wife in New York whose husband, through her efforts, has obtained a license to practice medicine or law will be told that she has an interest in that license and a right to receive a portion of its value, the same wife in any other state of the United States will be told that she has no such right, as it is a right recognized only in the state of New York. While a wife in the state of New Jersey or Missouri will be told that she has no legal right to share in property that was acquired by her husband by gift or through inheritance, the same wife in the state of Connecticut will be told that she may have such a right. While a wife in the state of Ohio will be told that she has a right to receive support from her husband for their children until they attain the age of twenty-one years, the same wife in the state of Florida will be told that she is entitled to receive support for them only until they reach the age of eighteen. And we could go on and on.

What conclusions must be drawn from this? There are only two possibilities. Either we are correct in saying that it is naive to believe that the law embodies some ultimate wisdom and guarantees some necessary justice or, if it does, then wisdom and justice are very different in different states.

Nor is this the end of it. The idea that legal rules embody what is right and guarantee justice is undermined by more than the fact that the various states have such very different laws. It is undermined by more than the fact that the rules, even of a particular state, are not always the same and change from time to time. It is also undermined by the fact that it is not possible to apply these rules so as to get predictable results, let alone consistent ones. On the contrary, their application will produce very different results in almost every case.

Before we consider this, however, and so as to better understand the terrible limitations in the application of legal rules, it will be instructive to consider a different set of rules, one applied, not by the law, but in a different setting. Suppose, for example, that there is a supermarket in your community—we will call it Nationwide Food Service. Suppose also that it has three check-out counters, each equipped with very sophisticated equipment, to add up the cost of a customer's purchases. Suppose, finally, that we filled three carts with exactly the same items, and that we took each of those carts to a different check-out counter. What would our reaction be if the first cashier told us that the items in our cart totalled $160; the second, $213; and the third, $245. Would we be satisfied if we were told, in solemn terms, that the equipment employed by Nationwide was the state of the art, and was guaranteed to provide us with the correct result? Or would we report Nationwide to the Better Business Bureau? More importantly, would we continue to do our shopping there?

This, of course, is exactly the state of affairs with the application of legal rules. We may be told, in solemn terms, that they embody the wisdom of the ages, and that they will guarantee some necessary justice. Nevertheless, when these rules are applied by different judges, like the cash registers employed by Nationwide, they somehow produce very different results.

To illustrate this, let us consider awards made for child support. It was common knowledge in the past that awards of child support made by judges, not only within the same state and the same country, but even within the same courthouse, varied considerably. In fact, the tremendous disparity in child support awards, and what was considered to be the terribly inadequate level of all of them, became such a national disgrace that in 1984 the federal government enacted legislation to address the problem. This legislation required each state to establish child support guidelines to assist judges in making child support awards. Its purpose was to eliminate not only the terrible discrepancy in those awards but also their inadequate level.

Not only did this federal legislation charge each state with the responsibility of doing the same thing—to determine what was a fair and appropriate level of child support—but to a very large extent their thinking was influenced by the very same factors and considerations. In fact, it was largely influenced by one and the same study, the report of Thomas J. Espenshade, a senior research associate of the Urban Institute, entitled *Investing in Children.*

Having been charged with the same responsibility, and having been guided in the discharge of that responsibility by one and the same study, it would be natural to assume that the various states came to the same conclusion at the end of their journey. They did not, however. In fact, they did not even take the same road to get there.

To illustrate this, let us take the results that were reached in just four of the fifty states. In each instance, we will assume the same state of facts, namely, a family having two children where the wife is employed earning $25,000 a year and the husband $50,000. The children live with their mother, who pays $1,500 a year to have someone care for them after school while she is at work. Her unreimbursed medical expenses for the children cost her an additional $500 per year.

How much would it be fair for the husband to be obligated to pay, and the wife to have a right to receive, each week for the support of their two children? Not the same amount in any of the four states. In the state of Illinois the award would be about $160 per week. In Virginia, it would be about $213. In New York, it would be about $245. And in California, it could be any one of those amounts, and many more in between. Worse yet, in each instance the parties would be advised that the award was correct and that justice had been done.

All the polite and high-sounding talk aside, is there really any difference between Nationwide Food Service and Nationwide Legal Service? And if we would not do business with one, why would we do business with the other? It was one thing when we believed that what we were being given was the one and only right answer. It is quite another, however, when we examine those rules more closely and realize that they do not give us a better answer than we could have come to on our own. All that they do is give us a different one.

There are very important implications in this. If legal rules do not embody the wisdom of the ages and guarantee some necessary justice—if they are not the better ones—then it is appropriate to ask why it is necessary or even sensible for separating and divorcing couples to turn to them, particularly given the very incredible price, in terms of time, cost and emotional injury, that they will be asked to pay in the process. It is particularly appropriate to ask why they should turn to them rather than to employ the far more sensible procedures that are available.

Until now, divorce lawyers have been very successful in stifling this question. How have they managed to do this? By portraying legal rules not as the rules that Barbara and Bill will apply if they can't find better ones, but as the better ones. By portraying them as rights, and worse, as the vehicle whereby the wrongs that have befallen each of them in their marriage will be corrected and what is rightfully theirs secured.

In short, they have stifled the question by making the issue one of principle. After all, if what is at issue is a question of principle—if the object of our quest was the Holy Grail or the Lost Ark—we would not stop to question the cost. These are sacred objects, and even if our quest should take a lifetime, and cost a king's ransom, it would not be too much. But what if legal rules are not precious objects? What if they are only fool's gold? And suppose that they are not legal rights? Suppose they are really legal *penalties?*

In truth, of course, that is exactly what they are. If Barbara and Bill lose sight of the fact that what they must do—what the intelligent, responsible thing to do—is to somehow put aside the terrible feelings that so overwhelm them, and resolve the important issues in their lives on their own, the price they will pay for that will be to be brought before a judge who, in effect, will say to them, "You were not mature enough, and sensible enough, to put aside your hurt and anger and decide whether or not you should send your son to day camp this summer, and who should pay for it? That is all right. I have just decided it. Now go home."

Unfortunately, it is very hard for separating and divorcing couples to see this. After all, we have all been brought up to believe that "Everyone is entitled to their day in court," and the legal mythology that has been employed to persuade us that legal rules are legal rights has encouraged us in this belief. Nevertheless, while each of us may be entitled to our day in court, as anyone who has been there will tell you, there are few among us who are so ill deserving that we should ever be required to have to go there. Not if we have a choice.

THE FOURTH MYTH

Legal Rules Will Provide Separating and Divorcing Couples
With Answers to Their Problems
And Lawyers Employ Legal Rules
To Get Them Those Answers

If legal rules are not really rights in the sense that we think they are, and if they do not embody some ultimate wisdom or guarantee some necessary justice, why then should separating and divorcing couples look to them, or apply them, to resolve the problems in their lives? More importantly, why should they do this, rather than resolve them on their own? There is only one possible answer, and this is that the application of these rules will provide them with clear, expeditious answers to their questions, and will thereby solve their problems. Unfortunately, the law fails this test as well.

The irony is that separating and divorcing couples really know this. If this is so, why, then, do they still turn to lawyers and to the law? As we have seen, part of the answer lies in the fact that they have accepted the mythology that what is at issue in these proceedings are both justice and their legal rights. But it also stems from the fact that separating and divorcing couples do not really understand what legal rules are or, more importantly, how they are applied by lawyers.

If that mythology is to be exposed, therefore, it will be necessary that they understand not only what legal rules are, but, and more importantly, how they are applied. For if it is a myth that the law provides clear answers to the problems with which separating and divorcing couples find themselves confronted, it is an even more dangerous myth that lawyers actually employ legal rules for any such purpose.

Consider the following. Barbara has just been advised by Bill that he wishes to divorce her. Upset by his decision, and fearful of where that will leave her, she consults with an attorney and asks him the question that every woman asks, namely, "What are my legal rights?"

This, unfortunately, is not what her attorney hears. After all, he does not think that Barbara has come to him as a legal academician, or to pose intellectual questions. Rather, and given the adversarial nature of our legal system, what he assumes is that she has come to employ him as her legal champion. What he hears her ask, therefore, is, "How much can I get?"

In asking the question that she has, Barbara may assume that, like the rules of mathematics, legal rules are abstract principles that are applied to guarantee that the proper answer will be reached, and the problem will thereby be solved. However, that is not how her attorney views legal rules. From his standpoint, the substantive and procedural rules of the law are simply advantage and disadvantage cards in a game of legal chess. Nor is it his job to apply them dispassionately, to assure a just result. Rather, and given the very nature of our legal system, he believes that it is his job to play as many of these advantage cards as he can to advance Barbara's cause, and to throw down as many of these disadvantage cards as he can to impede Bill's progress. In short, he does not view his job to be to get what is *fair* for Barbara. He views his job to be to get what is *best* for her. And what does he believe is best for her? To get as much as she can.

And what is the attitude of Bill's attorney? Very much the same. Thus, and although Bill has come and asked his attorney what every man asks, namely, "What are my legal obligations?" this is not what his attorney hears. Again, viewing legal rules just as Barbara's attorney does, what he really hears Bill ask him is, "How little must I give?" For he, too, is interested in what is best for his client. And what does he believe is best for him? To give as little as is possible.

Needless to say, Barbara and Bill do not come away with the same answers. On the contrary, they are each given very different answers, despite the fact that they each asked the same question. In other words, when each lawyer was asked to do his arithmetic, and to add up Bill's obligation, they were both given the same numbers to work with—their respective ages, the length of their marriage, the number of their children and the dates of their births, their respective earnings and so forth. Nevertheless, given the way lawyers apply legal rules in our adversarial legal system, they came away with very different answers.

Unfortunately, neither Bill nor Barbara will give very much thought to this. Rather, their world of understanding will be bounded by the answers that they were given by their own attorneys. Worse yet, they will not only accept these answers as gospel, but also, as we have seen, as the expression of their God-given rights as well. If either of them should consult with more than one attorney, and if the second attorney has reinforced the opinion of the first, which is likely to be the case, this will only tend to harden Bill's and Barbara's attitude. Thus, if Barbara should learn that Bill has been given a very different answer than she received, her reaction will simply be to dismiss it as being irresponsible, and attributable to bias and, perhaps, even malice.

It is very important that separating and divorcing couples give more thought to this than history proves that they have. In fact, it is critical that they come to understand why it is, and how it is, that they are given such different answers to the same question by the separate attorneys with whom they have consulted if they are ever to free themselves from the tyranny of legal rules and the manner in which they are applied by adversarial lawyers.

Let us suppose that the problem that Barbara and Bill had was a mathematical problem rather than a legal problem. Let us further assume that the procedure they employed to get an answer was the same one that they had employed to get an answer to their legal problem, namely, to consult with separate mathematicians. What would have been the result? Assuming that both mathematicians were competent, Barbara and Bill would have come back with the same answer. In fact, we would be very surprised if they hadn't. After all, mathematical rules, if properly applied, should lead to one, and only one, answer. More importantly, it shouldn't make any difference whether it was Barbara's mathematician or Bill's mathematician who applied these rules. In fact, and since the proper application of mathematical rules can lead to one, and only one, answer, it wasn't necessary for Barbara and Bill to spend the time or money to consult with two—one denominated Barbara's mathematician and the other Bill's mathematician. One mathematician would have been sufficient.

Suppose, however, that the two mathematicians did not agree. In fact, suppose that they never agreed and that the answers given by Barbara's mathematician and by Bill's mathematician were always different? Although we might still cling to the belief that their problem was a mathematical one, we would be hard-pressed to understand what it meant to say that it had a mathematical solution—that it could be solved, and their problem ended, by the application of mathematical rules.

This is exactly the case with legal rules. As we have seen, and as we all know, a lawyer consulted by a wife and a lawyer consulted by a husband will literally never agree with one another. On the contrary, they will invariably give their respective clients very different answers to the same question. In fact, if we wished to parody the law, we could say that the only reason why Barbara and Bill have a problem in the first place is because their separate lawyers gave them such different answers to the same question.

Why would they have received the same answer from both mathematicians when they received such different answers from their separate attorneys? For the very reason that all mathematicians apply the same weight to the same numbers and employ the same procedures in dealing with them. For example, one does not say that the weight of five is one more than four, while another says that it is two more than four. Rather, they all attribute the same weight to the same numbers. Similarly, one mathematician does not add where another subtracts, or one multiply where another divides. Again, they all apply the same procedures. This is why mathematicians are able to give us clear and precise answers to our questions. And this is why they all agree on the answer and thereby solve our problem.

The same is not true of attorneys. There are a number of reasons for this. The first is that attorneys do not deal in numbers. They deal in factors. Or, to be more accurate, although Barbara and Bill each give their respective attorneys the same numbers—their ages, the length of their marriage, their incomes and so forth—their attorneys do not attach the same weight to them.

Let us illustrate this. In the state of New York, for example, there are eleven factors that must be applied by a court in determining whether or not spousal support is justified, and the amount and duration of that award. These factors are the following:

1. The income and property that each of them has, including any property acquired during the marriage, that was distributed to them at the time of their divorce;

2. The length of their marriage, their ages and health;

3. Their present and future earning capacity;

4. The ability of the party seeking maintenance to become self-supporting and, if applicable, the period of time and training necessary for this;

5. The reduced or lost lifetime earning capacity of the

party seeking maintenance as a result of having foregone or delayed education, training, employment or career opportunities during the marriage;

6. The presence of children of their marriage in their respective homes;

7. The tax consequences to each of them;

8. The contributions and services of the party seeking maintenance as a spouse, parent, wage earner and homemaker, and to the career or career potential of the other party;

9. The wasteful dissipation of marital property by either of them;

10. Any transfer or encumbrance made by either of them in contemplation of their divorce without fair consideration, and;

11. Any other factor that the court shall expressly find to be just and proper.

Unfortunately, and unlike the numbers used by mathematicians, these factors do not lend themselves to any clear or certain results. That is because they do not come with assigned weights. Rather, they have such weight as a court can be persuaded to give them. Thus, Bill's lawyer is free to argue that factor number four should be given the most weight, while Barbara's lawyer is free to urge that it is really factor number eight that is most important. In fact, the two attorneys can even base their arguments on the same factor—for example, the second—with Barbara's lawyer pointing to the fact that the parties have been married for almost twenty years in support of the conclusion that she should be given a substantial award of maintenance, and with Bill's lawyer pointing to the fact that she is only thirty-nine years of age to support the conclusion that she should receive no support at all. That is why it is not possible to add up the various factors applied by the law in the same way that mathematicians are able to add up a set of numbers. And that is why it is not possible for the law to give Barbara and Bill clear and certain answers that will solve their problems.

This may, at first, be difficult for us to accept. To begin with, that is not generally how we view the law. Furthermore, our experience tells us that the law does, in fact, provide clear and certain answers all of the time. For example, if we inquire of an attorney what the legal voting age is, he will tell us quite clearly that it is eighteen. Similarly, if we ask him what is the maximum speed at which it is lawful to drive, then, and except in those states where it is higher, he will tell us that it is fifty-five miles an hour. And all lawyers will give us the same answer.

Why is it that lawyers can agree on the answers to these legal questions but are not able to agree on how much support Barbara will receive, or for how long she will receive it? The reason is that the law is able to give us clear answers only in those situations, such as the age at which it is legal to vote, when the answer is the same for everyone. That is why the law is able to tell a wife what percentage of her husband's estate she is entitled to inherit. Because, and subject only to the number of children their husbands have, all wives are entitled to inherit the same percentage, whether they have been married for a long time or a short time, whether they are young or old and whether they have been good wives or bad wives.

The amount and duration of support that a wife will receive is not the same for all wives, however. On the contrary, it is different for every wife, and in each instance the determination must be based upon the unique facts in each case—in other words, based upon all of the factors that are irrelevant when the question is, instead, what percentage of her husband's estate a wife is entitled to receive upon his death. Thus, in a situation such as this, it is not possible for a lawyer to provide a clear answer in the way that a mathematician can. Since the factors applied by the law can add up differently, and can therefore produce different answers, all that a lawyer can do is to indicate the *range* of possible answers. In other words, while a mathematician can tell us that the answer is forty-seven, and only forty-seven, the most that a lawyer can tell us is that it is probably somewhere between forty-four and fifty.

There are certain important implications in this that have not generally been appreciated. Moreover, they bear upon the idea that legal rules are the instruments whereby justice will be accomplished. For, like Heisenberg's Law of Indeterminacy in physics, there is an inherent conflict between the law's ability to give clear answers and, at the same time, to do justice in a particular situation. The clearer the answer is—as the case with a wife's interest in her husband's estate—the less fair will be the result. Conversely, the fairer the intended result—as is the case with the amount of support a particular wife will receive upon her divorce—the less clear the answer will be.

This has particular significance for separating and divorcing couples. For while the law prior to equitable distribution may not have been very fair—in the sense that a wife was not entitled to share in any of her husband's property, and a husband was obligated to support his wife forever—it was very clear. Unfortunately, and to the very extent that our equitable distribution statutes attempt to be fairer—to judge each wife on her own merits—to that very extent their application is less clear. That is why, when we consult with any number of mathematicians, we will be given the same answer while, when we consult with any number of attorneys, all that we will come away with is so many different opinions.

While this may explain why it is not possible for lawyers to give precise answers in the same way that it is for mathematicians, it does not explain why the answers (opinions) that will be given to Barbara and Bill by their respective lawyer will vary, and be as far apart, as they will. To understand this, it is necessary to add another consideration to our discussion, and that is the very different goals that mathematicians and lawyers have, and the very different masters that they serve.

In the previous example, when Barbara and Bill con-

sulted with separate mathematicians, each mathematician viewed his function to be the same, namely, to determine the correct answer. Nor did it make any difference to the mathematician employed by Barbara that she hoped that he would conclude that the sum was a large one, any more than it made any difference to the mathematician employed by Bill that he hoped that it would be a small one. Thus, and although Barbara and Bill each paid the mathematicians they employed for their services, neither mathematician was particularly concerned with whether Barbara or Bill was pleased with their answers. Why was that? Because neither mathematician felt that he had any allegiance to his client, even though it was his client who was paying him for his services. Thus, while both mathematicians felt that they had an obligation to provide Barbara and Bill with the correct answer, neither felt that he had an obligation to provide them with an answer that they would like.

If their mathematicians' allegiance was not to them, then to whom was it? Ironically, it was to the procedures that they employed in dealing with the numbers, and to all of the other mathematicians in the world who employed the same procedures. Thus, while they were not concerned with whether or not Barbara or Bill liked their answers, they were very concerned that all other mathematicians in the world did. That is why all competent mathematicians come to the same conclusion. And that is why it is not necessary to consult with two or three, and why any one good mathematician will do.

The same is not true with lawyers. Attorneys do not employ the various factors considered to be relevant by the law to arrive at an answer. Nor, as Barbara and Bill may have assumed, do they employ them to solve their problem. Rather, they employ them to make a case—in fact, the best possible case for their clients that they can. Unlike mathematicians, they are not seeking the truth or looking for the right answer. For a lawyer, the right answer is not some abstract conclusion. It is whatever a judge or jury can be persuaded that it is. From the standpoint of Barbara's lawyer, therefore, if he can persuade the court to give her support in the amount, and for the duration, that he told her it was her right to receive, then the answer that he gave to her was the right answer.

Thus, and unlike her mathematician, Barbara's attorney's allegiance is to Barbara, and to her alone. This is why he could not care less how other lawyers view the arguments he makes on her behalf or the conclusions to which he comes, least of all Bill's lawyer. This, too, is why the range of answers that will be given by Barbara's attorney and by Bill's attorney will vary as much as they do. And this is why the application of legal rules will not help Barbara and Bill to solve their problem or to resolve their dispute. The application of legal rules will not solve their problem for the simple reason that their lawyers do not apply them for this purpose.

But where is truth, justice or equity in all of this? Surely these are what the law intends and what lawyers are trained to seek. Mythology aside, nothing could be farther from the truth. Thus, and while lawyers may like to flatter themselves that what they are doing is adding to the common good, there are few of us who believe that. Lawyers, after all, do not add to the size of the pie. They simply fight over how to divide it. Thus, and notwithstanding all the talk of justice and equity, neither attorney could care less whether the agreement is fair. After all, they are not trying to get what their clients deserve; they are simply trying to get everything that they can for them. This being the case, it is worse than mythology that two lawyers, neither of whom could care less whether the agreement is fair, will somehow conclude a fair agreement. It is a travesty. And, as Barbara and Bill will learn, they will each pay dearly for it.

THE FIFTH MYTH

An Agreement Will Be Concluded Between the Parties
By the Skillful Negotiations Conducted by Their Attorneys

As we have seen, the application of legal rules did not provide answers to the problems that Barbara and Bill have. In fact, in the adversarial world in which these rules are applied, it is fair to say that legal rules actually create these problems. How are Barbara's and Bill's attorneys going to solve the problem that they have created for the two of them? The mythology is that they are going to do this by using their skill and experience to negotiate an agreement between the two of them. The truth is that, having given Barbara and Bill such very different answers to the same questions, and then having sprinkled legal holy water on them by characterizing these answers in terms of legal rights and entitlements, they have left themselves very little to negotiate. In fact, they have made their job all but impossible.

Let us consider the situation again. When Barbara consulted with her attorney and asked him how much support he thought that she could expect to receive, he could have told her that if he played his cards carefully, and with a little bit of luck, he might be able to persuade the court to give her between $325 and $350 a week for nine to ten years, but that, if the game did not go as he had hoped, the court might be persuaded by Bill's attorney to give her only $225 to $250 a week for no more than six or seven years. That is not what he told her, however. What he said, or at least what she heard, was that she was entitled—that it was her legal right—to receive the higher amount for the longer period of time. Worse yet, since Barbara walked away believing that what she had heard was the expression of her God-given rights, she also left feeling that she would be a fool to take less. Unfortunately, the answer given to Bill by his attorney left him with the same impression, namely, that he would be fool to give her more.

What, then, has been the effect of Barbara's and Bill's attorneys having characterized the answers that they gave to them in terms of legal rights and obligations? It has been to dip them in legal cement. And, as they will quickly find, it is very fast-drying cement, at that.

How will Barbara's and Bill's lawyers extricate the two of them from the predicament that they have created? Again, the mythology is that they are going to do this by falling back upon their skill and experience. Unfortunately, it is much easier to say this than it will be to demonstrate it, particularly when our common sense tells us just the opposite. After all, what is it in the experience and skill of Bill's attorney that will enable him to persuade Barbara's attorney, who has just told her that she is legally entitled to receive between $325 and $350 a week for at least ten to twelve years, to accept only $225 to $250 a week for no more than five or six? And even if, by some legal sleight of hand or other hocus-pocus, he could be so persuaded, how is he going to go back and get Barbara to accept it?

The answer is that he is not. That might not have been the case if the answers that Barbara and Bill had been given by their attorneys had represented simply a legitimate difference of opinion—Barbara being told, for example, that she could expect to receive approximately $300 a week for a period of eight or nine years and Bill having been told that he could expect to be obligated to provide her with support of approximately $275 per week for between seven and eight years. If that had been the case then, and even though their answers may have been framed in terms of legal rights and obligations, the two attorneys, falling back upon their skill and experience, might have been able to effectuate the necessary compromise and thereby solve the problem. However, the answers that they gave to their clients were so different, and so disparate, that whatever skill and experience they may have has been rendered almost useless.

There is something else that will make the problem even more difficult to solve, and that is that when Barbara's and Bill's attorneys sit down to discuss a possible settlement, neither of them will state his true position—neither attorney will propose to the other what they have just told their respective clients that they should expect to receive or to give.

As we have seen, and contrary to the accepted mythology, legal proceedings do not represent a process of informed, logical reasoning. Rather, and in the adversarial world in which legal rules are applied, they represent a game of legal chess. All of the polite talk of justice, rights and equity aside, the object simply is to get as much as you can and give as little as you have to. The rules are that there are no rules. Rather, it is anything that the law will allow, and as Barbara and Bill will quickly learn, the law will allow a great deal.

Adversarial proceedings, then, are simply a form of legal warfare. The object of all wars is the same: to end up a winner and to avoid being a loser. The best result, of course, is to bring your adversary to his knees and to obtain an unconditional surrender. And though lawyers forever defend adversarial proceedings, and attempt to underscore their virtues, by repeated reference to ethical considerations that are built into the process to protect the parties, the truth is that war is war and that these rules, which are little more than the etiquette of the game, are more honored in their breach than they are in their observance. Notwithstanding the trumpeting of high-sounding phrases, therefore, in a world such as this, where deceit is as likely to be rewarded with success as is honesty, truth is not necessarily a virtue. In a world such as this, exaggeration quickly becomes the order of the day.

When Barbara's and Bill's attorneys meet, therefore, neither can afford to state his actual position. Rather, Barbara's attorney informs Bill's that what Barbara expects to receive is between $375 and $400 a week for a period of eleven or twelve years. Bill's attorney, for his part, replies that he is not prepared to pay her more than $175 to $200 a week for between four or five years.

Will the two attorneys then sit down and, employing their skill and experience, negotiate the diffences between their respective positions? The answer is no, for if they had little to talk about before, they have even less to talk about now. After all, it is one thing to bridge the distance between the shores of New York and New Jersey, separated only by the Hudson River. It is quite another to attempt to bridge the vast ocean of difference that exists between the positions taken by Barbara's attorney and Bill's attorney.

What then will the two attorneys do? Sometimes nothing, at least nothing that is very constructive. Just as the generals of opposing armies know that they have little, if anything, to discuss between themselves, so, too, the legal champion whom Barbara has hired knows that it is pointless for him to suggest to Bill's attorneys that he give in to her demands. Even if they do meet at this stage of the proceedings, all that will happen is that they will each lay their demands on the table and then leave, confirmed in the belief that, given the position taken by the other, any further discussions between them would be pointless.

The bargaining positions taken by Barbara's and Bill's attorneys have done more than just to increase the distance between them, however. They have also poisoned the atmosphere. What, after all, is Barbara to think when her attorney returns and tells her that Bill has offered her support of between only $175 and $200 a week for no more than four to five years, when he has previously told her that she is legally entitled to received between $325 and $350 a week for at least nine to ten years? Does she simply explain this to herself as being a function of how legal rules are applied, and how the game is played, in the adversarial world of legal chess, and dismiss it as being no more than an initial bargaining position taken by her husband? Unfortunately, she does not. Rather, and like a painful antiseptic applied to an open wound, Bill's offer only adds insult to her injury, exacerbating further the very painful and difficult feelings with which she is struggling. When Bill's attorney returns from the meeting and reports back to him what Barbara's attorney has demanded, his reaction will be the same.

Assume No Risk

While the legal cement that Barbara's and Bill's lawyers have dipped them in will be a problem enough, there is another consideration that will add further to their difficulty and make it even more difficult for their attorneys to effectuate a settlement between them. Moreover, it is one that has not generally been appreciated as it should be. Ironically, it is a factor that will stand in the way of a settlement between them even when they are in basic agreement. That factor is risk.

Risk is everywhere. It is an inherent part of our lives, and there is simply no way to eliminate it. We are at risk when we walk out of our homes. We are at risk when we get into our cars. And we are even at risk when we walk up the stairs, or take the elevator, to go to our attorneys' offices. How do we deal with these risks? As best we can. But since we can never eliminate them, we try not to think about them. For if we did, we would be so anxious, and so paralyzed by fear, that it would be impossible for us to go about the business of our lives.

Lawyers, however, are obsessed with risk. Like hypochondriacs who see germs and the possibility of illness at every turn, lawyers are overwhelmed by the thought of risk. For a lawyer, the perfect world is a risk-free world. This being so, the motto he lives by, and the counsel he gives, is to "Assume No Risk." Thus, and although Barbara and Bill may not have been legal hypochondriacs when they entered their attorneys' offices, they will become them by the time they leave.

Let us illustrate this. In fact, to demonstrate how a lawyer's obsession with risk only adds further weight to the tremendous burden that Barbara and Bill will have in seeking a legal solution to their personal problems, we will take as our examples not areas in which they are in disagreement but, rather, areas in which they are not—at least until they get into their attorneys' offices.

When Bill first met with his attorney, he advised him that, although he and Barbara had not resolved many of their differences, they had come to an agreement that their two children would continue to live with Barbara in their home until the youngest graduated from high school. They had even agreed upon the periods of time that the children would spend with Bill and the fact that, when the home was sold, the proceeds would be divided equally between them.

Pointing to the motto emblazoned on the wall above his desk, Bill's attorney advised him that there was a problem. It was wonderful that he and Barbara had agreed when he would have the right to be with his children on weekends and during the week. But there was still a problem. Suppose Barbara remarried or got a new job and decided to sell the home and move away. How would he be able to see his children then? Similarly, it was wonderful that he and Barbara had agreed that, when their youngest child graduated from high school, their home would be sold and the proceeds equally divided between them. But suppose Barbara does not continue to maintain the home properly, and allows it to fall into a state of disrepair, as a result of which the home depreciates in value and Bill receives less than he deserves. Bill's attorney cannot let him assume these risks. He therefore proposes that their agreement contain a provision obligating Barbara to live within a certain distance of their present home, to assure Bill's continued access to his children. He also proposes that their agreement require her to maintain their home in its present state of repair, to assure that it will not decline in value. That will better protect Bill from these risks.

What will be the reaction of Barbara's attorney to these suggestions? More importantly, will he permit her to accept them? The answer, of course, is no; for he too has as his watchword "Assume No Risk." Suppose that the occupation of Barbara's new husband requires that she move and live at some distance from her present home. And suppose that Barbara, who, of necessity, will now have to live on a somewhat reduced budget, is unable to maintain the home as the two of them did while they were married. How can he permit Barbara to assume these risks?

Nor does it make any difference how large or small the risk is, or how legitimate it would be to assume it. Without question, Barbara will have great difficulty in maintaining the home in its present state of repair in the future. That the home may decline in value (or not appreciate at the same rate that it otherwise would) is thus a real danger. But if that happens, it will not be because Barbara purposely let the home go. It will be because there just was not enough money to do all of the things that had to be done. It is unfortunate that Bill will have to assume this risk, but is it inappropriate that he do so? It makes no difference. His lawyer wants no part of it.

And what of the question of Barbara's possible relocation? To be sure, Barbara has no intention of moving from her home. Nevertheless, and while it is not very likely, it is a possibility. More importantly, and unlike the depreciation in the value of his home, which involves only money, this may substantially interfere with Bill's ability to maintain an ongoing relationship with his children and they with him. It is understandable, therefore, that Bill should be concerned about this. It makes no difference. Barbara's lawyer will have no part of it. This being the case, he cannot permit her to enter into an agreement that contains any restriction on where she may live with the children, just as Bill's attorney cannot permit him to enter into an agreement without such a restriction.

Ironically, although Barbara's and Bill's attorneys are obsessed with risk, they are also colorblind to it. In other words, while they are highly attuned to certain risks, they are almost oblivious to others. This, too, is something that is not generally as appreciated as it should be. Nor, therefore, will Barbara and Bill be aware of the effect that it will have upon their attorneys' negotiations and how it will tend to block any agreement between them.

In the real world, where risk is everywhere, it is impossible to avoid it. The question, therefore, is not whether our decisions involve possible risk. The question is how great that risk is and whether we feel that the intended benefits are such that they justify our assuming it.

Unfortunately, and being legal hypochondriacs, lawyers do not live in the real world. They live in lawyer-land. This being the case, their vision is very distorted. And because it is distorted, they do not actually see all of the risk that they are so on guard against. Nor, therefore, do they ask themselves all of the important questions that they should. Thus, while Bill's attorney is concerned about the risk to Bill were he to enter into an agreement that did not contain a restriction on where Barbara may live with their children, and while Barbara's attorney is equally concerned about the risk to her were she to enter into an agreement that contained such a restriction, neither attorney will ever concern himself with the question of where his client will be left, and the inevitable risks that will entail, if they are not able to conclude any agreement at all. Being colorblind when it comes to risk, lawyers somehow never see this as a problem. (It is as if a motorist, who is about to cross over a busy thoroughfare, looked for oncoming cars in only one direction, and not in the other.) What makes this all the more ironic is the fact that the danger that Barbara and Bill face in not being able to conclude an agreement, and in having to continue the war, is a present danger, and a real danger, while the risks with which their attorneys are obsessed are only future possibilities and, even then, usually only remote ones.

Why is it that lawyers are so colorblind to risk? To understand this, and to understand why the double standard that lawyers have when it comes to risk will make it so difficult for Barbara's and Bill's attorneys to conclude an agreement between them, it is necessary to consider yet another legal myth. This is the myth of the reasonable man.

The minute that they entered law school, Barbara's and Bill's lawyers were introduced to the reasonable man. More importantly, they were instructed that from that point forward all human conduct, including even their own future conduct as attorneys, had to be judged by the standard of the reasonable man. Suppose a lawyer is consulted by someone who complains that he slipped on a banana peel that was inadvertently thrown on the floor by one of his co-workers. Would a reasonable man have done this? The answer is no. The co-worker was therefore negligent, and liable for the injuries that the attorney's client sustained as a result.

It is a very reasonable test. Nevertheless, there is one problem with it. The reasonable man is never negligent, and never makes a mistake. Thus, while he may represent a very commendable model, he, too, lives only in lawyer-land and not in the real world. In short, he is only a legal fiction. Nevertheless, and once they enter the world of the law, real people in the real world, who are fallible and whose conduct is therefore less than perfect, will be judged against this (ficticious) legal character. And, as they will find, he is a hard master because he admits to no errors and tolerates no mistakes.

This is all well and good with banana peels. After all, we all know that they belong in garbage cans and not on the floor. There is thus no excuse for them to be there. But what of the rest of human conduct, which is inherently fallible, no matter how hard we may try? It makes no difference. A sentry may carefully walk his watch, observing every sign of possible danger, ten thousand times. Nevertheless, should he lapse, even ever so slightly, on the ten-thousand-and-first night, and there be consequent injury as a result, he will be found guilty. Nor will his perfect performance on each of the preceding ten thousand nights serve to exonerate him. Rather, he will be judged by the reasonable man based on how he walked his watch on that night alone.

The standard in lawyer-land is thus a very exacting one. In a world such as this, therefore, one cannot afford to take chances; for to take a chance—any chance—is to run the risk of making a mistake. And since everything that we do involves risk, in a world such as this it is much safer to do nothing than to do something. If you do something, you run the risk that you may make a mistake. However, if you do nothing, you can always fall back on the excuse that you purposely did nothing to avoid doing something and thereby run the risk of making a mistake.

Barbara's and Bill's lawyers know this. In fact, it is their expertise. Bill's lawyer, therefore, does not want Bill to sign an agreement that will permit Barbara to move with their children anywhere she wishes any more than Barbara's lawyer wants her to sign an agreement containing a provision that she will maintain the home in its present state of repair. In fact, and rather than assume any such risk, they would each prefer that they sign no agreement at all.

Put aside for the moment the fact that if a truce is not called, and an agreement concluded, the legal warfare that Barbara and Bill are engaged in will continue, with the consequent damage that this will inevitably entail. Isn't it in Barbara's and Bill's interest that they be protected from these risks, and isn't it their attorneys' responsibility to do just this? The answer is no, even though, given how each attorney defines his role and his obligation, it will seem otherwise. It may well be that in the legal world of the reasonable man in which Bill's and Barbara's attorneys live, risk is like a hot potato that neither of them wants any part of, and that each attempts to throw into the other's hands. In the real world where Barbara and Bill live, however, and where risk is everywhere, you cannot avoid it. Nor can you simply pass it along to someone else. All that you can do is share it. In the context of their dispute, that means that Barbara may have to agree to accept some restriction on where she may live with their children, and that Bill may have to accept the fact that this restriction will have to be eased in certain circumstances. At least that is what they will have to do if they are ever going to be able to conclude an agreement.

Certainly Bill's and Barbara's attorneys must know this. Why then do they raise all of these obstacles to an agreement between them? It might be flattering to attribute this to their zealous advocacy of their clients' interests. Unfortunately, this explanation will not do. To be more accurate, it is only half the story. It may well be that Bill's attorney does not want him to sign an agreement that will permit Barbara to move wherever she may wish with their children because that will subject Bill to the risk that he may not get to see them as he would like. But Bill's attorney is not only concerned with the risk in this to Bill. He is also concerned with the risk in this to himself.

Suppose that Bill's attorney, in order to break the impasse that is preventing Bill and Barbara from concluding an agreement, recommends that Bill accept a provision in the agreement permitting Barbara to move with their children, relying on the fact that Barbara really has no intention of going anywhere, and that there is little likelihood that she will, and that she is insisting on such a provision simply because she fears being so restricted. Where does this leave

Bill's attorney should Barbara later change her mind? It leaves him subject to criticism from Bill, and this leaves him at risk.

But why is Bill's attorney at risk from Bill? After all, Bill is on his side. It makes no difference. In war you can be killed by friendly fire almost as easily as you can by the enemy. In fact, a lawyer's client is potentially his worst enemy. After all, Barbara is little threat to Bill's attorney. Since he does not represent her, she cannot sue him for malpractice. But Bill can, and his attorney knows this. Bill's attorney can therefore take no chances with Bill.

Suppose that Barbara does move, and Bill is thereby deprived of the easy access that he now has to his children. Will Bill remember that this was a legitimate risk that he decided to take? Will he remember that it was done to bring the war to an end, and to thereby establish some peace between them? Will he even take into consideration the many other risks that he safely assumed, let alone the risks that Barbara also assumed, perhaps to her detriment? The answer, of course, is no. Bill's attorney will be judged by his own standard, that of the reasonable man. And, as we have seen, the reasonable man admits no mistakes, and accepts no excuses.

This is why it is mythology, and worse—a travesty—for Barbara's and Bill's attorneys to suggest that, by employing their skill and by falling back on their experience, they will be able to conclude an agreement between them. For in setting their sights so high, all that they have done is to dig a very deep hole for themselves. And by insisting that they can only get out of it if they do not expose themselves to any risk in the process, they have made it all but impossible for them to do so.

Attrition

If it is not by means of skillful negotiations that Barbara's and Bill's attorneys are going to be able to solve the problem they have created for them and bring them to an agreement, how, then, will it be accomplished? After all, divorce lawyers boast that in the vast majority of instances they are able to conclude an agreement between the parties, and that probably no more than five or ten percent of their cases are ultimately resolved by the court. If this is so, how then are these settlements concluded? The answer is that they are concluded through attrition.

While it is true that most matrimonial matters are ultimately settled—usually at the courthouse steps and sometimes even in the midst of the trial—and that very few are actually decided by the court, it is disingenuous for divorce lawyers to suggest that they were concluded through negotiations, let alone that their skill and experience had anything to do with it. It is even more dishonest of them, in taking credit they ill deserve, to deny just how dependent they were on those adversarial legal proceedings, or that it would have been impossible for them to effectuate a settlement without them.

Let us consider this. Having given Barbara and Bill such very different answers to the same question, their attorneys have done more than just to leave them with a problem. In the process, they have also left each of them with a terribly false level of expectation. At least on some level their attorneys know this. They also know that no amount of skill or experience is going to be able to budge either Barbara or Bill from the fixed positions that they have been encouraged to take. This is why, contrary to conventional mythology, their attorneys rarely attempt any serious negotiations at the outset. As a courtesy, they may meet with one another to find out just how far apart they are. In most instances, however, they will not even bother to do this, knowing just how pointless such a meeting will be. Thus, while the parties may believe that they have retained their attorneys to negotiate an agreement for them, and that they are actively engaged in that undertaking, if they were to look at their attorneys' time records, they would be shocked to see how little time has been spent negotiating, or even preparing to negotiate, anything. How, then, has it been spent? In the famous war of papers that divorce lawyers traditionally engage in.

Having little faith in the skills they so highly tout, and knowing that no amount of persuasion will budge their opponent from his or her position, each attorney feels compelled to turn to self-help and to pressure. Up until now, Bill has been paying all of the household bills. In fact, he has expended most, if not all, of his earnings for this purpose. Bill, of course, cannot continue to make the same payments following his and Barbara's separation and divorce that he made during their marriage. However, the amount that he has proposed is not only far less than this, but an amount that is clearly inadequate for Barbara's and their children's needs, and she, just as obviously, cannot accept it. Thus, and although Barbara may also very much want to get on with the matter, to do so at the expense of accepting Bill's offer is, from her point of view, like signing her own death warrant. And so she does nothing, and that is where they remain.

After some time, and frustrated by Barbara's lack of movement, either Bill or his attorney feels compelled to take matters into his own hands. This means applying pressure to Barbara. If their problem is that they are unable to effectuate a settlement because a settlement means that Barbara will get less than she is presently receiving, perhaps the answer is to make the proposed settlement offer larger than the amount that she is now receiving. Not by increasing the settlement offer, but by decreasing the amount that Bill is now voluntarily giving to her. And so Bill decides to bring pressure to bear upon Barbara by dramatically reducing the amount of money that he has been giving to her up to this point.

But Bill is basically a reasonable, decent man. How could he do such a cold, calculated thing? It will not be difficult. Although there may not, as yet, have been any overt act of aggression between them, the atmosphere has already been so poisoned with anger and frustration that there will be more than enough excuse to do it, and reasons to justify it, when the time comes.

As with the assassination of the Archduke Ferdinand at Sarajevo that began the First World War, the isolated event that ignites the ultimate conflagration between the two of them soon disappears as but a spark in a huge fire. Nor is it necessarily the same spark that ignites the fire in each instance. It makes no difference. Whatever the initial cause, every action breeds a reaction in a never ending cycle that soon grows so out of control that it is almost impossible to trace it back to where it all began, let alone to stop it. Worse yet, and since it will take many months, and perhaps even years, for the fire to burn itself to an end, it may get out of hand, and cause serious damage, before it is extinguished and the matter finally brought to a conclusion.

It is at this point that the court's assistance is usually invoked and the lawyers' famous war of papers begins. For obvious reasons, Barbara cannot simply permit Bill to reduce the money he is giving to her to whatever level he wishes. To begin with, she cannot live on it. Nor, in most instances, does she have available funds that she can employ to supplement it. Even if she had, however, she may be reluctant, and even fearful, to resort to them, as she looks upon these monies as being her only security, which will then slowly but surely be eaten away. Besides, why should she use her own funds to support herself and their children when that is Bill's obligation?

There is a second, and equally important, reason why Barbara cannot permit Bill to put this pressure on her. Unless she finds a way to relieve it, then, and in the long days ahead, she may find herself weakened and forced to give in. So she, too, resorts to self-help. Unfortunately, there may not be that much help at hand. In that case, and often without being fully aware of what she is doing, she may resort to their children, who are subtly, and sometimes not so subtly, drawn into the conflict. And now they both feel compelled to seek the aid of the court.

There is another, and less obvious, reason why either Barbara or Bill will invoke the court's assistance. Husbands and wives engaged in adversarial legal proceedings soon find themselves involved in a great deal of positioning. Why is this? Because, unlike mathematicians who will all come to the same answer, judges are given a great deal of latitude in their decision making. This means that their answers can vary greatly. Nor is it very easy to check them. With mathematicians, since they all follow the same procedures and since these procedures lead to one and only one answer, it is easy for one mathematician to check the answers of another to make sure that they are correct. With legal answers (legal opinions), however, and since there is a whole range of answers that are acceptable, it is not that easy. To make matters worse, a reviewing judge, unlike a reviewing mathematician, does not believe that he can put himself in the same position as the judge who made the initial determination. For this reason, and for others that have more to do with the administration of a judicial system than the correctness of any particular determination, a great deal of deference is given to the first judge's determination.

Understandably, each of the parties is therefore very concerned about how the judge who is assigned to the case will view it. As a result, they are forever positioning themselves so that they will appear in the most favorable light. That is why the year of a husband's divorce is traditionally his worst year financially, and why, regardless of how bright his past may have been, the predictions as to his future are always dim and often worse. It is for the same reason that wives are traditionally instructed by their attorneys not to seek employment while the matter is still pending, and why they go to such lengths to present themselves as being almost totally incapable of providing for their own support.

Thus, in the game of legal chess that divorce lawyers

play, Barbara cannot permit a situation that might suggest that she had been able to provide for herself and her children on the less-than-adequate payments Bill had given to her. Nor can she put Bill in a position where he will be able to make this argument. It is therefore necessary that she make application to the court for an order directing him to pay her more.

As Barbara feels compelled to make this application, so, too, Bill feels compelled to oppose it. To begin with, he has brought pressure on her for a reason, namely, to force her to back down and to modify her position, thereby bringing some movement to discussions that have grounded to a halt. If the court grants her application, and in effect relieves Barbara of the pressure that he has applied to her, Bill will be back where he started. Just as importantly, he cannot permit Barbara to use a favorable award to put pressure on him to settle the matter on her terms. Worse yet, if the court directs him to provide more suitable support for Barbara and their children, and if he complies with the court's order, he may well leave the court with the impression that he is capable of paying support in this amount on a permanent basis.

While Barbara and Bill, and their respective attorneys, may attempt to employ the court as both a shield and a sword in their ongoing struggle, and as a means of containing it and keeping it from getting out of hand, as they will find, it will prove to be of far less help than they had hoped. Turning to the court is not like building a secure wall of protection against a swelling sea—once the wall has been constructed, we are forever safe. It is more like attempting to secure oneself against a leaking dike by plugging the holes with one's fingers. Thus, all that our efforts will provide us with is, at best, temporary relief, and we must forever be on our guard against new dangers.

In terms of our last example, there are three possible outcomes. The award granted by the court will please Barbara, it will please Bill, or, as is more often the case, it will please neither of them. Whatever the outcome, however, its effect will not have been to bring about an end to the war. At best, it will only effectuate a temporary lull. Whether it will serve as a basis for a new skirmish, or produce a Mexican standoff, it is but one more chapter in the ongoing saga. Even if Barbara is successful in obtaining an adequate order of support, her victory may only be a short one. Bill may appeal it. He may later make a motion to modify it. Or he simply may not comply with it. To be sure, Barbara may have her remedies. But these remedies are always administered after the fact, and are far less effective than they are generally touted to be.

It is not enough that the relief afforded by our legal system is less than effective. It is also slow moving, and very costly. As everyone knows, it takes two lawyers at least a month to waltz around the floor together just once. And, as anyone who has been invited to watch the dance will tell you, it is an extremely expensive performance. (Ironically, it is the very fact that it moves so slowly, and takes so long, that accounts for the fact that it costs so much.) To make matters worse, those who commit themselves to the dance find that they have no way to stop it. They are thus condemned to continue to pay the piper for his tune, whether they can afford it or not, until either it comes to an end or they give up listening.

This is how the matter is finally concluded when the parties turn to the law and to adversarial proceedings. Not by skillful negotiations, as lawyers like to boast. Not by the self-help that the parties feel compelled to engage in. And not by the costly war of papers that their attorneys substitute for real answers to their problems. Rather, they are settled through attrition. Worn down, frustrated, and financially exhausted, one or both of the parties finally gives up and gives in. In the beginning, it was more important to get it right than to get it done. Having lost faith that they will ever get it right, they would now at least like to get it behind them. As we stated earlier, not uncommonly, the

ultimate settlement is effectuated on the courthouse steps
and, sometimes, even in the very midst of the trial. While
their lawyers will add this settlement to their lists of successful negotiations, it was not effectuated by their skill
and experience. It was not even bought at the very high
price that the parties were each required to pay. It was
achieved only because they were finally forced to confront
the unreality of their expectations and to accept, not what
was right but, what was possible.

Unfortunately, the final settlement of which Barbara's
and Bill's lawyers will boast, and for which they will take
such ill-deserved credit, will not come without a price. For
if their attorneys started out by giving them unrealistic levels of expectation, they will end up leaving them with equivalent levels of disappointment. That, and not justice, is the
sad legacy that they will be bequeathed for having accepted
legal mythology. That, and the fact that they will be left as
hurt and angry when they end as they were when they
began.

THE SIXTH MYTH

Separating and Divorcing Couples Retain Separate Lawyers
Because Separate Lawyers Will Protect Them

As we have seen, it is not the fact that separating and divorcing couples look to the law and to legal rules to resolve their disputes that causes them to have the problems that they do. Rather, it is the fact that these rules are applied in adversarial legal proceedings—in proceedings that view the parties as being adversaries and that therefore make adversaries of them. Perhaps the answer, then, is not to discard legal rules, but simply to apply them differently. After all, it may well be that legal rules are only the rules we apply when we can't find better ones. But if Barbara and Bill are unable to agree on the better ones, why wouldn't it make sense for them to employ them? They may not embody the wisdom of the ages or guarantee that justice will be done. They may not even be the right rules in the sense that Barbara and Bill think they are. But—and putting aside the question of deciding who will keep the newer of two television sets—they are certainly better than flipping a coin or playing a game of chess.

If this is the case, perhaps the answer is for Barbara and Bill to apply them, but in a different way. Not as weapons in a legal tug of war, but as an impartial arbiter when they are unable to agree between themselves. How can they do this? By consulting, not with two lawyers, separately, but, together with one. In other words, if the only thanks that they will get in consulting with separate lawyers is to come away with two very different answers, perhaps the solution is to consult with a single attorney and come away with but one. To be sure, the attorney will not be able to give them an answer in the same sense that a mathematician would, for as we have found, if Barbara and Bill insist on getting the answer they would be given by a judge in a court of law, then they are going to have to go to court to get it, since no two lawyers will agree on what that answer is. But this does not mean that a competent attorney could not give them a *range* within which they could expect a court's decision to fall. After all, what does it mean to be a competent attorney if a lawyer is not able to do this? More importantly, since the attorney they select will be attempting to give them an answer, and not make a case, we would expect the parameters of that attorney's opinion (the most and the least that Barbara and Bill could reasonably expect) to be close enough to facilitate an agreement between them and not, as was the case with the positions taken by their separate lawyers, so far apart as to make an agreement all but impossible.

Unfortunately, this simple solution sends lawyers into a frenzy. In fact, they speak and act as if what they had been confronted with were a subversive plot aimed at undermining our most precious values, not to mention God, country and motherhood. Worse yet, they meet in great ceremony to discuss how they should best deal with this very dangerous idea, as if the issue were the protection of the common good.

To understand the legal profession's attitude toward this rather sane, simple solution, it is necessary to understand its defense of our legal system. As every law student learns in his and her first week of law school, ours is an adversarial system of law. From the standpoint of that system, what is at issue in each instance is, first, the determination of the facts and, then, the proper application of the law to those facts. In the public's eye, these two, separate considerations have generally become melded into one. The question is,

"Is the defendant guilty or is he innocent?" (Or, to be more technically accurate, "Has his guilt been proven under the law?")

The purpose of our adversarial system of law is to answer this question. More·importantly, and in defense of our adversarial system, it has generally been regarded as the best instrument that has been devised for this purpose. At the pinnacle of this system is the judge, or jury, whose function it is to decide the facts. Given the realities of life, however, the trier of facts, as the judge or jury is called, comes to this task with certain potential disabilities. To begin with, they may be limited in their investigative abilities, and in the resources available to them for this purpose. They come burdened by the limitations of their own intellectual abilities and the constraints of their individual points of view. They bring with them their own biases and prejudices. Then too, and being only human, there is always the danger that their decisions may be affected by the thousand-and-one considerations that add up to human fallibility. This being the case, it became necessary to add two other participants to the proceeding. They are known as the prosecuting attorney and the defense attorney, and, as we will see, it is their presence that characterizes our legal system as an adversarial one.

What is the function of the prosecuting and defense attorneys? Theoretically, it is to aid the trier of facts, be it the judge or jury, in its ultimate determination. More importantly, it is to act as a counterweight to the inherent limitations that the trier of facts brings to its task. And, as with all systems, it works best when each of its component parts (in this case, the prosecuting and defense attorneys) correctly performs its individual functions and when there is a proper balance between them. Concomitantly, it will not work correctly if any of the participants ignores his assigned role or, worse, abandons it in favor of that assigned to one of the other players. Iago may well prefer to read

Othello's lines. But the drama will not properly unfold unless all of the players—villains and heroes alike—are true to their respective roles.

As an actor's ultimate commitment is to the play, so, too, the commitment of both the judge, the prosecuting attorney and the defense attorney is to the judicial process. It is this commitment that explains, and in turn justifies, the ability of an attorney in our adversarial system to defend a person accused of a crime, even one whom he strongly believes to be guilty of the offense. It is not his job to make this determination. It is his job to present all of the facts, and to marshal all of the arguments, that he can in support of the conclusion that his client is innocent (or, to be more accurate, in support of the conclusion that the prosecuting attorney has not proved his guilt under the law) to assure that the judge or jury, in carrying out its function and in making its determination, has not overlooked any of these facts or arguments, or failed to give them their due significance. It is then for the judge or jury to determine whether the facts and arguments presented by the prosecuting attorney or the defense attorney are more persuasive. It is not a perfect system—and the presence of appellate review is both an acknowledgment of this fact and a safeguard built in to increase the likelihood that justice will be done. But, as its champions maintain, in the real world, it is the best system that we have been able to devise to assure that the truth will win out.

To understand fully the legal profession's opposition to the suggestion that one attorney will do as well, and perhaps better, than two, there is a second aspect of our adversarial system that must also be mentioned. While the prosecuting and defense attorneys' primary responsibilities are to the judicial process—which is why they, as well as the judge, are known as officers of the court—over time they have also developed a special relationship with, and have been charged with a responsibility to, their respective clients. (In the United States, because attorneys have become so identified with their clients and their clients' interests, it is very difficult for us to see them has having any other role. It is even harder to see their primary identification as being to the court and to the judicial process. It is easier to see this in Great Britain, where there has always been a greater distance between a barrister—the attorney who will represent the client in court—and his client, where the barrister initially has no direct contact with his client and where he is generally retained, not by the client himself, but by the client's solicitor.)

The identification of an attorney with his client's interests derived from the fact that the two parties had very different hopes and expectations with respect to the outcome. (It is from this that the principle of the parties' conflicting interests derives.) In short, each party wishes to win the case, which by definition is impossible and a contradiction in terms. This being the case, and since it is impossible for one attorney to champion the interests of two people, both of whom wish to win, his identification had to be with only one of them.

Over time, there developed a set of ethical rules, known to lawyers as the code of professional responsibility, that defined an attorney's obligation to his client in such an adversarial world—prohibitions against disclosing information that has been given to him by his client in confidence, against representing interests in conflict with those of his client's, and so forth. In fact, in an important sense, these ethical proscriptions are intended to mediate between the attorney's own conflicting interests—his interest as an officer of the court in the judicial process and his interest as the advocate of his client in his client's best interests. (This inherent conflict of interests is heightened in criminal proceedings. One of the things that a defense attorney—although he is an officer of the court—must do on behalf of his client is to protect him from the terrible power of the state, and sometimes the abuse of that power, through the vehicle of those very judicial proceedings that are supposedly intended to assure that justice will be done.)

Unfortunately the logic, and the force of the argument, that supports the edifice of our adversarial judicial system has been so long accepted that, like the emperor's new clothes, it no longer seems appropriate to question it. Worse yet, any attempt to do so is met, not with any rational argument or defense, but with the kind of irrational hysteria with which one is greeted when one attacks a sacred cow that has outlived its usefulness, and whose ancient origins of sanctity can no longer be remembered. Question it we must, however, if we are to save future generations of separating and divorcing couples from being roasted on our adversarial system's sacred skewer of conflicting interests.

Whatever important truth our judicial system is supposed to protect when what is at issue are questions of constitutional privilege or the guilt or innocence of a person accused of a crime, there is no such important truth involved in a couple's separation and divorce, certainly not one that would justify the terrible price that separating and divorcing couples, in resorting to our adversarial system, have been forced to pay to get it. To be sure, and in traditionally viewing divorce as a quasi-criminal proceeding that has as its purpose the determination of the guilt and innocence of the respective parties, our judicial system has acted as if what was at issue was some important truth. It is not, however—a fact that the law is only now belatedly beginning to understand, let alone to acknowledge. Rather, what is at issue, as we have seen, is simply the fact that a couple's decision to divorce has left them with certain practical problems that they are unable to resolve on their own, as they have in the past.

To be sure, one or both of the parties may believe that what are at issue in their divorce are certain truths about their marriage, and that the proper function of their divorce is to establish these truths. Except in the rarest of instances, however, this is not the case. This being so, in encouraging separating and divorcing couples in this misguided fantasy, our adversarial system has not done them a favor. On the contrary, it has led them down a blind alley in which they can only get lost. Worse yet, it has only added to the pain they will experience as an inevitable by-product of their divorce.

If it is not to determine some important truth about their marriage and their divorce that would justify Barbara and Bill turning to the law and to legal proceedings, what then is it? This brings us to the second cornerstone of our adversarial legal system and to the second line of defense that it invokes to justify the use of adversarial proceedings. And that is that the parties are *at risk*. Being at risk, they therefore need separate lawyers because separate lawyers will protect them.

This justification for turning to adversarial proceedings is a rather curious one. It is curious because, in advancing it, lawyers unwittingly acknowledge just how inadequate are all of the other reasons they have advanced to persuade separating and divorcing couples to turn to the law and to legal procedures to help them. Be that as it may, it is only mythology that Barbara and Bill need separate lawyers, because separate lawyers will protect them. On the contrary, the truth is that, having retained separate lawyers, they will now each find themselves in need of protection.

Consider the following. Barbara is informed by Bill that he wishes a divorce. Fearful as to where that decision will leave her, and encouraged by her Greek Chorus of well-wishers that she must immediately retain counsel, she calls and makes an appointment with an attorney for that purpose. From Barbara's standpoint, that may seem both a natural and an appropriate thing to do. After all, all that she is doing is consulting with an attorney to find out what her legal rights are.

Unfortunately, that is not how it will appear to Bill.

From his standpoint, Barbara and her attorney will be meeting secretly, privately, behind closed doors. Nor, despite the fact that he will probably be the principal topic of conversation, has Bill been invited to attend the meeting. In fact, were he to learn about it, and to appear unexpectedly, Barbara and her attorney would be very embarrassed by his presence, and the meeting would come to an abrupt end. What can Bill think? Certainly not that Barbara has gone there for the purpose of planning a party for him! It may be a surprise, but it will hardly be a surprise party. All that he can assume, therefore, is that Barbara and her attorney are meeting together, and planning together, to take him for all that they can. This being the case, Bill decides to consult with an attorney himself. What is Barbara's reaction when she learns of this? There is only one reaction that she can have, and that is that it was a smart thing that she went out and got herself a good lawyer first.

It is not just that Barbara and Bill have gone out and consulted with separate attorneys that is the problem, however. It is that the meeting that they had with their attorneys took place in a particular context. Lawyers in our society, after all, perform their services in a certain setting, one that is based upon certain assumptions. Ours is an adversarial system of law. Nor do lawyers apologize for this. On the contrary, they are very proud of this. There is one problem, however, and this is that our legal system, and the lawyers who function in it, proceed on an assumption. And that assumption is that Barbara and Bill are adversaries. As a result, each lawyer views his role as being to enter the lists, and to do battle with the other, to champion his client's cause and to protect his interests—his legal rights. Whether Barbara and Bill really were adversaries, in the sense that the law would have it, when they began, is a question that could well be debated. It is also now irrelevant. For, like every self-fulfilling prophecy, in assuming that they are adversaries, this is exactly what they will become.

All of the players in the drama, attorneys and clients

alike, know this. It is not something that they necessary verbalize. They may not even consciously be aware of it. But it is in the air, nevertheless. Thus, when Barbara and Bill meet with their respective attorneys, they do more than seek legal advice. They begin to plan, not only what they will do, but also how they will prepare themselves for, and protect themselves against, what the other may be planning to do. For, like Barbara, Bill is also meeting with his attorney, secretly, privately, behind closed doors. And Barbara has not been invited either. Ironically, Barbara does not view the meeting she had with her attorney in this light. Rather, she sees it as being both a natural and an innocent act. Nevertheless, the same natural and innocent conduct, when engaged in by Bill, will be viewed as hostile, and as posing a dangerous threat.

There is one further aspect of this context which must be mentioned. While, at first blush, it might seem that when Barbara turns to a lawyer and to the law, she has entered a safe place, what she really has done is to step into a no man's land. And Barbara instinctively knows this. Like the criminal of old who, in transgressing society's rules, puts himself outside the protection of the law, Barbara knows that, in turning to adversarial legal proceedings, she has put herself in the line of fire. And Bill knows this too.

Why is it that, in turning to the law, Barbara and Bill each feel that they have exposed themselves to lawlessness? Because they know that in hiring separate attorneys, and in electing to do legal battle with one another, they have entered an arena in which the object is simply to get as much as one can and to give as little as one has to and where the rules are that there are no rules and that it is anything the law will allow. They also know that it is a world in which no holds are barred, and where it is each man for himself. Thus, although the mythology is that these legal proceedings will protect them, the truth is that in turning to these proceedings they will now each need protection. Worse yet, they will find what protection they will get from the adversarial system they have turned to to be very inadequate. The irony, again, is that they really know this. They also know that, more often than not, the help they will be given by the law will be too little, too late. In fact, at least in part, this is the reason that they will each eventually feel compelled to resort to self-help to improve their respective positions and to do for themselves what they are afraid the law will not do for them.

There is yet a further irony in all of this. When Barbara and Bill decide to go into the lists and to do legal battle with one another, what they are really doing is entering the land of the spear chuckers. Nevertheless, when they embark upon the process of choosing a champion who will do battle for them, they invariably ask the wrong question. When Barbara meets with her attorney for the first time, one of the things that she would like to know is just how good an attorney he is. To put her at ease, he recites for her the fact that he is a matrimonial specialist and has been engaged in the practice of the law for more than twenty years, all of which attests to the fact that he can chuck a spear fifty yards and hit the target accurately. He then recounts to her the fact that he is also a member in good standing of the Family Law Committee of the American Bar Association as well as a Fellow of the American Academy of Matrimonial Lawyers, all in proof of the fact that he can perform this incredible feat twenty times in a row. And so, armed with this information, Barbara leaves, assured that she has retained an expert spear chucker. Unfortunately, Barbara did not ask the right question. What she should have asked this attorney was just how good a spear *catcher* he was. After all, what does she think that Bill's attorney will be doing while her own attorney is taking aim at him?

This brings us to the worst ill consequence of this misguided mythology. For what has been the effect of Barbara's assumption that Bill's decision to divorce her has left her in need of protection and that the law will provide her with that protection? It has been to make Bill, rather than her divorce, the problem. When she entered her attorney's office, it was because she was getting a divorce. This was her problem. By the time she left his office, however, this was no longer the case. By the time she left, it was Bill who was her problem.

This was illustrated by a couple who had turned, not to adversarial proceedings, but to mediation, in an attempt to resolve their problems. In this instance, it was the husband who was seeking the divorce. His wife, who was extremely emotionally insecure, was very threatened by his decision, and by where that would leave her. Curiously, and although her insecurity was evident throughout, she first expressed her concern only after the two of them were well into the mediation. She was not sure, she told the mediator, whether she felt comfortable in mediation, or whether it was really suitable for her, because she had seen how men acted when they decided to divorce their wives. How had she seen this? the mediator asked. Two friends of hers had gotten divorced recently, she said, and she had observed how their husbands had acted and what they had done. At the mediator's prompting, she gave a chapter-and-verse account of their conduct and how they had acted toward their wives. Had her husband been guilty of any of this conduct? the mediator asked. No, the wife answered. In fact, and as the mediator well knew, he had gone out of his way to assure her that, unlike her friends, she had nothing to fear from her husband. Turning to the wife, the mediator suggested that maybe she really did not know how men, and women, acted when they got divorced. What she really knew was only how they acted when they turned to adversarial legal proceedings.

Unfortunately, this fact is not generally appreciated. The things that men and women habitually say and do when they are in the process of divorcing are so well known, and so well documented, that we have come to accept them as being natural by-products of the divorcing process. It is not, however, as those who have turned to procedures other than adversarial ones have learned. Without question, the decision to divorce unleashes painful, and terribly destructive, feelings that tend to overwhelm one or both of the parties—and we will have more to say about this at a later point in time. But these feelings do not necessarily have to lead to the kind of conduct that has all too often characterized divorce in the past. To be sure, if these feelings are fanned in the fires of an adversarial, life-and-death struggle, then they will get out of hand and do the terrible damage they invariably do. Thus, if separating and divorcing couples continue to buy legal mythology, and march off mindlessly to do legal battle with one another, then they will continue to be caught up in the vicious cycle that, in assuming that they are adversaries, makes adversaries of them. However, if they turn instead to procedures that are designed to prevent these destructive feelings from getting out of hand, and to help them to better control them, they will learn what countless numbers of couples have already learned, namely, that this conduct is not a by-product of the divorcing process, as legal mythology would have it. It is only a function of the adversarial procedures they have been persuaded to employ to effectuate that divorce.

THE SEVENTH MYTH

The Couple's Divorce Was Caused by the Fault
Of One of the Parties
And the Law's Function
Is to Punish Him for His Misconduct

The factors that bring a couple to the point of divorce make it difficult, and at times impossible, for them to resolve the issues that confront them as effectively as they have in the past. However, this does not mean that they will not be able to resolve these issues. It means only that they may be unable to do this on their own. This is attested to by the increasing number of separating and divorcing couples who, with but a little bit of help, have been able to conclude agreements between themselves without going off and doing legal battle with one another. If this is so, why do so many separating and divorcing couples continue to buy legal mythology and turn to adversarial legal proceedings? More importantly, why do they do this when they know full well what is in store for them?

To understand this, it will be necessary to consider certain other aspects of the very complex mythology that support adversarial legal proceedings. In particular, it will be necessary to focus our attention, first, on how this mythology is supported by the very feelings that make it so difficult for separating and divorcing couples to resolve the issues with which they are faced and, second, on how adversarial proceedings fuel these feelings.

To do this, we will examine two of the tenets of this

mythology. The first of these holds that one of the parties is responsible for the failure of the marriage and that, at least in part, the purpose of legal proceedings is to punish the guilty party. The second, which is in a sense a corollary of the first, holds that the application of legal rules, now called legal rights, will accomplish this, as they are the instruments that will effectuate justice between the parties.

Let us begin with the concept of fault. Traditionally, divorce was granted only when one of the parties was found to be guilty of conduct that so violated an essential aspect of the relationship that it was felt that the other party should be relieved of his or her obligation under the marriage contract. Thus, conduct that was viewed as grounds permitting one of the parties to obtain a divorce became a divorce occasioned by the misconduct, and therefore the fault, of the other. As a result, divorce actions tended to resemble quasi-criminal proceedings, the object of which was first to determine and then to punish the guilty party.

The punishment was meted out in two ways. First, the innocent party was granted a divorce. Second, the guilty party was sanctioned. This sanction could be in many forms. For example, until 1968, the law of the state of New York was that a husband or wife whose spouse was granted a divorce against him or her was not permitted to remarry during the other's lifetime. That was the penalty meted out to the guilty party—to the party whose conduct was deemed to be the cause of the divorce. More commonly, however, the sanction was an economic one. Thus, our divorce laws not only provided that fault could be considered by the court in awarding spousal support. In some instances, they directed that the guilty party could not be given any support at all, regardless of how needful he or she was, or how long they had been married.

The tremendous increase in the rate of divorce that took place in this country beginning in the early 1960s effected a tremendous change in our laws; and state after state adopted no-fault divorce laws permitting married couples to terminate their marriages without a showing of fault. Now, all that was necessary was for one of them to demonstrate that there had been an irretrievable breakdown in their relationship. Similarly, and particularly with the enactment of equitable distribution laws by the various states during the same time period, the idea that alimony was to be granted as a reward, or imposed as a punishment, was gradually discarded. This was reflected in the fact that many of these statutes changed the term denoting spousal support from *alimony* to *maintenance*. It was also reflected by another change. Rather than being permanent—and to do away with what had become known as alimony drones—spousal support, now termed rehabilitative maintenance, was to be awarded long enough only to enable the party receiving it to become self-supporting.

Unfortunately, the change in our divorce laws had more to do with our acceptance of the reality of divorce than with any better understanding of it. Put another way, the change in our divorce laws was principally an acknowledgement that marriage could no longer be viewed as being necessarily a permanent relationship. Just as importantly—and this is true of all equitable distribution laws—it was, by and large, an attempt to come to terms with the economic implications of this fact. When marriages end as a result of death, it is only necessary that our estate laws are fair to the surviving spouse. If they now end principally in divorce, however, it becomes necessary to make our divorce laws more equitable—to make an appropriate financial adjustment to reflect the fact that the accumulated wealth and earning capacity of husbands and wives was traditionally unequally divided between them.

While our present divorce laws may reflect a greater acceptance of the reality of divorce, they do not, at the same time, represent a more sophisticated understanding of it—of why marriages fail and the factors that lead to their demise. As a result, the mythology that divorce is occasioned by the misconduct, and therefore the fault, of one of the parties is still with us, and many state statutes still permit, and in some instances require, the court to consider fault when distributing property or awarding spousal support. More importantly, the idea of fault still informs the popular understanding of divorce and, in doing so, continues to fuel the mythology that causes separating and divorcing couples to turn to the law and to adversarial legal proceedings.

But isn't divorce, in fact, occasioned by the misconduct of one of the parties? After all, we all know men and women who have been divorced by their spouses either because they committed adultery or were guilty of cruelty to them. But we also know husbands and wives who did not divorce their spouses even though they were guilty of the same conduct. More to the point, we have known husbands and wives who divorced their spouses despite the fact that they were guilty of neither. It will therefore not do to attempt to explain divorce as being caused by this conduct, or at least to explain it based upon this conduct alone.

There is another, and an even more serious, problem with this simplistic understanding, however, and that is its failure to make the very important distinction between the factors that cause the relationship between husbands and wives to erode and the conduct that one or both of them engage in once that erosion has begun. Without excusing such conduct, and certainly without attempting to justify it, the fact remains that most of the conduct that has traditionally been seen as being the cause of divorce—the conduct that the law recognized as constituting fault—is usually conduct that husbands and wives engage in *after* they become unhappy or dissatisfied with their relationship, not the conduct that causes them to become unhappy or dissatisfied with it. Put another way, the conduct that the law has traditionally recognized as constituting marital misconduct is more often than not the *symptom* of the marriage's demise, not, as legal mythology would have it, its cause.

This is not to suggest that the conduct in question is not very painful to the offended party. Nor is it to suggest that it is not the source of a great deal of friction between the parties, or that it does not hasten the marriage's demise. It is simply to say that it is not a sufficient explanation of why people divorce. It does not explain why marriages persist for years and years, despite this conduct. It does not explain why the divorce is just as commonly initiated, not by the offended party, but, by the party whose conduct is supposedly the cause of the marriage's failure. And, as we have noted, it does not explain why marriages end in divorce despite the absence of any of the conduct that legal mythology would point to as its cause.

Legal mythology notwithstanding, married couples do not get divorced because they are good people or bad people. They get divorced bcause they are very different people. As one well-known therapist has observed, all marriages are mixed marriages in the sense that they bring together two people who have very different histories, characteristics and expectations. What their marriage represents is their ongoing act of negotiating these difference over a lifetime of personal development, change and, at times, even tragedy. Marriages that persist—those that we call successful—are those in which the couple is able to negotiate these differences successfully over the period of their life together. Marriages that fail—those that end in divorce—are those in which the couple is not able to do this, and in which the resultant friction leads to terrible disappointment and hurt and, ultimately, to the conduct that we simplistically ascribe to be the cause of their divorce.

When these negotiations are successful, a husband and wife will each be able to see the other in his or her wholeness. In fact, when they are successful, even failings and limiting traits can be viewed through the feelings of affection that each one of them has for the other. In these instances, these traits may even appear, not as irritants, but as amusing characteristics. On the other hand, when marriage negotiations are unsuccessful, these same traits will be viewed as fatal crimes. In fact, it will become difficult for either of the parties to see the other except through these very limiting facets that these irritating traits increasingly tend to present.

In the end, almost all that one or both of the parties will be able to see will be these extreme differences in character, these areas of friction that so sharply divide them. Unfortunately, these character differences are not viewed simply as this. On the contrary, the terrible frustration and irritation that they have caused the injured party have made these irritations appear to be grievous crimes. For, in time, these traits tend to deny him even the minimum conditions under which he feels he can continue to live. He is left angry by this fact and just as angry that, in order to change it, he is going to have to end his marriage and, in effect, to throw over the very structure of his life. To complicate matters further, it is difficult, and at times impossible, for the injured party to see, let alone to accept, his own role in what has happened—to see that the problem is as much one of how he reacts to the other's trait—how it affects him—as it is as to whether the offending trait is the terrible crime that he makes it out to be. His hurt, his anger and his resentment over where all this has left him are simply too great to permit this.

These are the feelings that one or both of the parties is experiencing, and that at times overwhelm them, at the time of their divorce. To complicate matters further, and as we have noted previously, their hurt, anger and at times their despair tend to be expressed through conduct that only further fans the flames of these very destructive feelings. In fact, and being unable truly to understand the basis of the conflict between them, the parties each tend to focus upon this offending conduct as being the cause of their divorce. If these factors have caused one of the parties to look beyond the marriage for emotional support, the terrible damage that this does to the other's self esteem, and the sense of betrayal that he feels, only deepens the pain and feelings of resentment.

As we noted earlier, legal mythology does more than feed on these painful feelings. It also fuels them. How does it do this? First, by reinforcing the injured party's sense of having been wronged, and, second, by encouraging him to believe that the function of the law and adversarial legal proceedings is to punish his spouse for the crimes, whether real or imagined, that he believes have been committed to him in the marriage.

To be sure, the change in our divorce laws over the last twenty-five years has put a large dent in the idea that the purpose of divorce proceedings is to reward one of the parties or punish the other. However, the atmosphere that surrounds adversarial divorce proceedings is still heavily charged with this idea, and divorcing couples are still encouraged to view this as one of the functions of adversarial proceedings. For while the enactment of equitable distribution, with its emphasis upon the economic realities of marriage, may have tended to de-emphasize *fault,* and with it the mythology that previously fueled adversarial proceedings, it has introduced a new element that fans these adversarial fires even further.

What, after all, is equitable distribution all about? It is about dividing the pie. Prior to the enactment of equitable distribution, there was nothing to divide. If property was owned by one of the parties during the marriage, it was owned by him as well upon his divorce. And a court had absolutely no power to do anything about that.

Equitable distribution changed this. As we have seen, courts are now empowered to give one of the parties an interest in the property acquired by the other during the marriage—and in some states, even if it was not. Since that division is always between husbands and wives, the effect of these statutes, unfortunately, has been to fuel what was already the unfortunate tendency of our divorce laws to see disputes between husbands and wives in terms of a class struggle, thereby promoting an almost Thurberian war of the sexes. After all, equitable distribution did more than to declare that the pie would now be divided. It also set forth the rules that courts would apply in making that division. Unfortunately, and since one set of rules could favor one of the factions in this class struggle and another set the other, equitable distribution also heralded the politicalization of divorce, with women's groups and men's groups vying with one another to apply legal rules either to benefit their respective constituencies or to change them when they did not. Thus, and while men and women were not born natural enemies, our divorce laws, and the mythology that supports adversarial legal proceedings, have nevertheless tended to fulfill the prophecy of that assumption.

What has been the effect of this? It has been to encourage separating and divorcing couples to look to their divorce as the occasion to right the wrongs, whether real or imagined, that they believe have been done to them in their marriage, and to legal rules as the instruments to accomplish this. If proof be needed of this, it will be found in the language, more graphic than responsible, that attorneys all too often employ in describing to their clients what it is that they intend to do to their husbands or wives.

Does it make any sense to lead divorcing couples to believe that this is one of the purposes of the law and of legal proceedings? After all, what is at issue in these proceedings is not whether one of them will be sentenced to prison for ten years but, instead, such mundane questions as with whom their children shall live, what support one of them will be required to pay to the other and how their property will be distributed. If this is the case, what sense does it make to cause them to lose sight of this? Worse yet, what purpose is served in encouraging them to view their divorce as the occasion to right past wrongs or to settle old scores?

The answer, of course, is that it serves none. Common

sense is enough to tell us this. There is no future in the past. Nor, ultimately, is there any solace in the very painful feelings, tied to the past, that separating and divorcing couples cling to. Since it is possible only to get lost in the terrible feelings that so overwhelm them, what they must do is to find a way to let go of them, and to put them behind them. This is the proper purpose of divorce—to get it done.

As we have seen, legal mythology sends out a very different message. The object of divorce is not to get it done; it is to get it right. Thus, and rather than being urged to sit down sensibly and resolve the issues with which they are faced, separating and divorcing couples are instead encouraged to believe that what is at issue are questions of principle, of right and wrong, and to run off to do battle with one another to vindicate them.

It makes no difference that they are being sent on a fool's errand. Nor does it matter that what they will get will be, at best, a phyric victory. It does not even matter that no one will stop to assess the cost and inevitable damage, let alone to ask whether it is worth it. If they persevere, and see it through to the end, they will be vindicated. And what will that reward be? Nothing but a piece of paper—a legal talisman—attesting to their spouse's guilt and their own innocence.

The tragedy is not in the fact that they will be denied what they had been promised—that they will not be rewarded or their spouse punished as they had been led to believe. It is in the fact that they will be denied what they should have received. What they needed was help to go forward, and help to turn their backs on the past—to conclude their marriage and to effectuate some emotional closure to the painful feelings that are associated with it.

This is not what they will be given, however. On the contrary, in accepting legal mythology, they will be left with just the opposite. As we have seen, the legal procedures to which they have been encouraged to turn will make a resolution of the practical problems with which they are faced more difficult, not less difficult. Moreover, it will leave each of them as hurt and as angry when they finish as they were when they began. But the real tragedy of adversarial legal proceedings is that it will not have served them by getting it right, as they had been promised. It will just have made it that much more difficult for them to get it done.

THE EIGHTH MYTH

Divorce Lawyers Want to Avoid Litigation
And Will Only Institute Suit as a Last Resort

Divorce lawyers forever insist that what they would really like to do is to resolve their clients' differences and to settle their cases rather than to litigate them. Just as responsible statesmen maintain that they would prefer to employ the skills of diplomacy and will turn to war only as a last resort, so, too, divorce lawyers repeatedly assure their clients that their aim is to get them a negotiated settlement.

This raises a question. If what everyone supposedly wants—lawyers and clients alike—is to conclude a peaceful settlement and to avoid lengthy, costly litigation, why, then, do husbands and wives invariably find themselves marching off to do legal battle with one another?

The answer, unfortunately, is a rather complicated one. In fact, there are a number of answers—a number of considerations—that account for it. First, while divorce lawyers may say that they would prefer a negotiated settlement— and for obvious reasons they are under a great deal of pressure to take that position publicly—the truth is that they do not view litigation, as the general public does, as being necessarily undesirable. After all, they are lawyers, and that is how disputes traditionally have been resolved by the law and by those who have turned to it. And that is what they have been trained to do.

Second, and perhaps more important, lawyers do not see negotiations and litigation as being "either/or." Rather, as war is considered to be an extension of diplomacy, so, too, litigation is considered to be an extension of negotiations. In fact, there is an even closer relationship between litigation and negotiations than there is between war and diplomacy. For while we resort to war only when diplomacy fails, litigation is commonly seen as a means to initiate negotiations, or as a device to resort to when negotiations, already underway, stall or come to an impasse. In short, lawyers do not necessarily view litigation as an alternative to negotiations. Rather, negotiations and litigation are more commonly viewed as two aspects of the same process.

The tendency to see litigation as part of the negotiating process is reinforced by another factor. With disputes between nations, if peace settlements fail, the matter is taken out of the hands of the diplomatic corps and put into the hands of the military. This has the effect of making the distinction between diplomacy and war very sharp and very clear. This distinction is also reinforced by the fact that there is an implicit understanding that a declaration of war, like Caesar's crossing the Rubicon, is generally irrevocable. From that point forward, there is no turning back, and it is either victory or unconditional surrender.

The same is not true with litigation, however. First, in most instances, the same attorney who had been the client's advocate at the negotiating table will now be his representative in the courtroom. Second, with warfare, once it is declared, the battle is not periodically interrupted to determine whether the two sides would like to return to diplomacy and the negotiating table. With matrimonial litigation, on the other hand, just the opposite is the case. Not only will the court interrupt the proceedings to inquire whether a settlement is possible, but, and on its own initiative, it may even intervene in an effort to effectuate one. Furthermore, the attorneys themselves—who, after all, are both the parties' chief negotiators as well as their litigators—are always at liberty to do this should they choose to. They are not even required to suspend or terminate the litigation for this purpose. Nor is it necessary for them to conduct these negotiation behind the scenes, or to rely on the good offices of third parties, as is so often the case in disputes between nations. Rather, the litigation, and those negotiations, can take place concurrently, with the attorney taking off one hat and putting on another as he switches roles.

Whose Fault Is It?

While these factors may explain why settlement discussions rarely proceed very far—particularly if they are not promising—before litigation is commenced, there is something that they do not explain and that is why, in probably a majority of instances, one of the attorneys will commence litigation even before any real attempt at negotiation has taken place rather than, as the canard would have it, only after it has failed. There are a number of reasons for this.

The first reason has to do with how it is that people come to the decision to divorce. Let us go back to Barbara and Bill. The conventional wisdom would have it that both of them decided that they wanted to divorce or, if that was not the case, that it was probably Bill's decision. Neither of these is true. The decision to divorce is rarely a joint decision, at least initially. On the contrary, it is usually the decision of but one of the parties. Moreover, and again contrary to the conventional wisdom, in the majority of instances, this party is the wife.

Barbara has been unhappy in the marriage for some time. Looking back, she may even feel that she has been unhappy from the very beginning. On the other hand, it is possible that the marriage was a generally satisfactory one for a number of years, and only later deteriorated. In any event, and while Barbara did not initially think of divorce, she has been giving it serious consideration for the last year to a year-and-a-half. More importantly, she has been preparing herself emotionally for this divorce in the process.

If Barbara has been as unhappy as she has been, it is

not possible for the marriage to have been an ideal one from Bill's standpoint, either. Nevertheless, he does not want a divorce. In fact, he is very much opposed to the idea. As a result, and although Barbara has, of necessity, signalled her discontent, Bill has either not seen these signals or, even when he has, has not taken them seriously. Bill, of course, knows, at least on some level, that there are problems in the marriage. Nevertheless, since he is either unwilling or unable to address these problems, let alone to accept their implications, his attitude has been that if he ignores Barbara's complaints, then perhaps they will go away. He has also proceeded on the assumption that, even if they do not go away, nothing will come of them. To make matters worse, and without being aware of what she was doing, Barbara has unwittingly encouraged him in this belief.

Like most people who eventually divorce, Barbara has not been of one mind. Thus, while there have been problems that have pulled her in the direction of a divorce, there have also been strong considerations that have weighed against that decision and have bound her to her marriage. (This is expressed in the well-known saying that people *stay* married for very different reasons than they *get* married.) As a result, and without being aware of it, Barbara has been sending out mixed signals to Bill—red lights that have signalled, "This marriage has to stop," and green lights that have signalled, "Well, maybe not." Worse yet, Bill has seen only what he wants to see. Thus, and while there have been far more red lights than green lights, Bill has been encouraged in the belief that, if he ignores the red lights and is patient, a green light will eventually come along. Up until this point at least, Barbara has not disappointed him. As a result, Bill has not taken her warnings, or even her threats, as seriously as he might have.

There is yet another consideration that contributes to this. Moreover, it is a consideration that will have significant implications at a later stage in the process. This is the fact that divorcing couples have very little understanding of just why it is, and how it is, that they have come to this point in their lives, let alone what their own role in the drama has been. How is it possible that they can only see the part that their spouse has played, and not their own? This is perhaps best illustrated by the well-known saying that husbands and wives very often divorce their spouses for the very reasons they married them.

People commonly marry other people who have comparable levels of maturity, but who have opposite defense systems. Unfortunately, it is the very differences that attracted one of them to the other that will very often later create the problem. Thus, a husband who was originally attracted to his wife because she was efficient and well organized may now complain that he cannot live with her because she is compulsive and obsessive. Similarly, a wife who was originally attracted to her husband because he was a very competent, take-charge person, who knew where he was going, may now complain that he is a "know it all" and a bully who tries to control her life. Will either Barbara or Bill see this, let alone how they bought into the problem? Unfortunately they will not. All that they will see is the trait in the other that is so irritating, and sometimes offensive, to them, and that they cannot live with.

Barbara will not get divorced because she wants to. She will get divorced because, in the end, that is all that she knows how to do. But Barbara did not get married to get divorced. Thus, and since she cannot see her own role in what has happened, or how she has contributed to it, she will tend to see herself as being the victim of what Bill has done or, to be more accurate, of what he has been unwilling to do. For years now, she has tried to get him to change. Not infrequently, she has even tried, usually unsuccessfully, to get him to join with her in dealing with, what to her at least, were the problems in their marriage. In truth, her complaints about Bill were not wholesale ones. On the contrary, there were only one or two characteristics, or shortcomings, of his with which she took issue. Nevertheless, these offending traits had so come to characterize her view of Bill and, therefore, their relationship, that she was no longer able to see him except through these limitations. More importantly, from Barbara's point of view, these limiting characteristics denied to her what had become the very minimum conditions for her happiness and, therefore, her ability to stay in the marriage. In time, and since Bill was unwilling to change, Barbara came to feel that she was left with no choice but to divorce him. Nevertheless, since this is not where she wants, or really ever expected, to be, she is very angry at Bill, whom she believes has put her there.

And what of Bill in all this? While Barbara has given him an account of her complaints, chapter and verse, *ad nauseam,* ironically, he does not really understand what she is complaining about. What, after all, has he done? He has not robbed a bank. He does not steal candy from children. In fact, if he is guilty of anything, it is simply in being who he is. Since, like all of us, Bill takes himself very much for granted, it is very hard for him to see what, if anything, he is guilty of, or, therefore, what Barbara has to complain about. If this is the case—and Bill, of course, believes that it is—then Barbara's complaints are unfounded, and are only in her head. (From Barbara's standpoint, of course, this demonstrates Bill's and her own total inability to communicate with one another, thereby confirming the validity of her complaints.)

Where does this leave Bill? If Barbara really has nothing to complain about, then there is nothing for Bill to do, except perhaps to suffer (and ignore) her complaints, as he has done so often in the past. From his standpoint at least, the very last thing that he should do is to take them seriously; for if he did, he might have to change. But he does not want to change. (Like Barbara, he also likes being who he is.) And since he has not committed any crime, he does not see why he should.

Matters between Barbara and Bill have therefore gone nowhere, except that, and as Barbara's upset has increased, they have gotten worse. Eventually, Bill is forced to confront the reality of Barbara's decision to end their marriage. But since Bill, too, did not get married to get divorced, the thought of a divorce that he does not want, does not understand and does not feel that he deserves does not sit well with him.

This, then, is the emotional climate that exists between them when Barbara consults with an attorney. While she and Bill are not emotionally at the same place—she has prepared herself emotionally for their divorce while he has not—there is one thing that they do have in common. They are both very hurt and, therefore, very angry. That anger has left few areas for any rational discussion. In fact, even previously safe areas have now become possible war zones, since the slightest exchange between them can serve as an excuse to unleash the feelings, just beneath the surface, that so overwhelm both of them. And this, of course, has left Barbara convinced that she will need legal assistance in order to resolve the issues between Bill and herself.

When Barbara retains an attorney, he tells her that he will begin by sending Bill a letter advising Bill that she has consulted with him for the purpose of obtaining a divorce. To signal his desire to resolve the issues between them without litigation, and to prevent it from getting out of hand, he advises Barbara that there will be nothing threatening in his letter and that it will simply be an invitation to talk. It makes no difference. No matter how polite it may be, Bill will not congratulate Barbara's lawyer on either his tact or his good intentions. Nor will he thank him. On the contrary, he will be offended by the letter, no matter what it says.

Unfortunately, this is not the worst of it. Falling back on the strategy that he has unconsciously employed these many years, Bill may simply ignore it. This may then be followed by a second letter, which will be a little less tactful and more to the point. This, too, Bill may ignore; not because he doesn't get the message, but because he doesn't care what Barbara does at this point. If this is the case, Barbara's attorney will send Bill a letter that he can't refuse to accept: It is called a summons. Thus, and before a word will have been spoken, legal warfare will have begun. To be sure, this summons is really only an invitation to talk. But it will be viewed as a declaration of war, nevertheless. And war it will be.

Tough Talk

While this may explain why litigation precedes formal negotiations in some cases, it does not explain why it occurs as often as it does. Nor does it explain why the litigation is commenced, not simply with the service of a summons— an invitation to talk—but with the service of a complaint as well—a chapter-and-verse recitation of all of the crimes, both real and imagined, that one of the parties contends the other has been guilty of. Nor does it explain why it may be accompanied, or quickly followed, by additional exchanges in the notorious war of papers that divorce lawyers have historically engaged in. To understand this, it will be necessary to consider certain other factors that influence how lawyers think and act.

When Barbara began to look around for an attorney, legal mythology told her that what she needed, and what she should make sure she got, was a "tough" lawyer. Legal mythology, and the Greek Chorus that is its messenger, never spelled out for Barbara why it was actually in her best interests to have a tough attorney. Nor did she stop to ask that question herself. It just seemed to make sense, and so she accepted it.

To be truthful, Barbara did not even really know what a "tough" lawyer did or, therefore, what it meant to be one. Nevertheless, she had some misgivings as to whether Justin Wright, the first attorney with whom she consulted, was. He seemed very knowledgeable and professional. He was also very even-handed and polite. Still, and although Barbara appreciated this, it also gave her some cause for concern. For while Barbara respected the fact that he was a gentleman and a professional, she worried whether those traits of his would serve her in the days ahead when the going got rough.

Urged on by her Greek Chorus, Barbara decided to put her misgivings on the table. She told Mr. Wright that she was impressed with his professionalism and felt very comfortable with him. Nevertheless, she had a concern. And that was whether or not he was tough enough to stand up to her husband. She even confided to him that she had been urged to make sure that she got herself a tough attorney and that she, too, felt that this was what she needed. And this was her concern.

Because he was everything that she had concluded he was, Mr. Wright did not attempt to defend himself. Nor did he even answer her question. Rather, he turned to Barbara and asked her a question of his own.

"Just how tough do you want your divorce to be?" he asked. "I want to assure you that I will be able to live through your divorce, no matter how bad it gets. That is not the issue. The question is whether you can. Remember, if you get yourself a tough attorney and if your husband gets himself a tough attorney, that doesn't mean that either of you will come out any better or with more. On the contrary, and since all that tough attorneys—attorneys who know only how to be tough—do is to get their clients embroiled in costly litigation, you will probably come out with less. Don't be fooled by glib talk. Tough is tough for everyone. Not just for your husband, but for you and your children as well."

The second attorney with whom Barbara consulted, Abel Wrong, was not such a gentleman. Nor was he as honest. He knew what people getting a divorce looked for in an attorney, and that was what he gave them. If they wanted tough, then tough is what they would get. Thus, if

Barbara came to Mr. Wrong believing that she had been used and abused by Bill, by the time she left him there would be not doubt left in her mind. And if she was of the opinion that what she needed was someone to protect her and to stand up to Bill, by the time she left Mr. Wrong's office she would not only be convinced that she was right, but also that he was her man. As the saying goes, actions speak louder than words. If tough is as tough does, what better way for Mr. Wrong to demonstrate this than to drop the first bomb—to serve Bill with a summons and complaint to show him that he means business. This, therefore, is what he tells Barbara he intends to do.

Barbara may have liked Mr. Wright, the first attorney with whom she consulted, better. She may even have felt more comfortable with him. More often than not, however, she will listen to her Greek Chorus and buy legal mythology. More often than not, she will retain Mr. Wrong.

Divorce Warfare

While all of these reasons may be sufficient to explain why divorce lawyers turn to litigation as often and as readily as they do, they still do not tell the whole story. Rather, there are other, and even more practical, considerations that must be taken into account.

Divorce proceedings are notoriously protracted, and there are a number of reasons for this. The first has to do with the fact that divorce proceedings have traditionally been viewed, not as the occasion to sit down and make sense of a difficult situation, but, as legal warfare. Wars, as we all know, are not won by the just or the virtuous. They are won by those who are the strongest and best equipped for the battle. Moreover, one can just as easily obtain victory by outmaneuvering or wearing down one's enemy as by defeating him. Thus, one of the parties may feel that it is in his or her best interest to protract the proceedings. Since attorneys, and the whole judicial process for that matter, seem to move at a snail's pace, it will take at least one year, and quite often longer, for the process to wend its way to a conclusion. With just a little bit of help, it can take considerably longer.

If this was true in the past, modern divorce law, with its requirement that there be an equitable distribution of the couple's property, has tended only to accentuate the problem. Under the old divorce law, a court had no power to distribute property owned by one of the parties to the other. This being the case, the value of the property in question, let alone its increase in value during the marriage, was rarely an issue. Under our modern divorce law, however, it is now critical. As a result, it is now necessary to place a value on all of this property—homes, stocks and bonds, businesses, retirement benefits, professional practices and in some states even degrees and licenses. This, in turn, has necessitated invoking the services of a whole host of persons—accountants, appraisers, brokers, actuaries—who had not previously been involved, or, if they had been, not to the same extent. The effect has been to protract the divorce process even further, at times interminably. This creates a problem for the two attorneys. While all of these matters could, theoretically, proceed without the court's intervention or even its knowledge, given the adversarial nature of these proceedings, in actual practice it does not work this way. Quite the contrary, and precisely because these proceedings are adversarial in nature, one or both of the parties will feel the need to seek the court's assistance.

There are a number of reasons for this. The first has to do with Barbara's and Bill's attitudes toward the law, which, rather ironically, are very ambivalent. On the one hand, and like all divorcing couples, they each want whatever they are legally entitled to. On the other hand, they are each afraid that what they are entitled to may not be as much as they would like, let alone need. This has traditionally caused divorcing husbands and wives to do many things with the truth—to hide it, to color it and to exaggerate it—but rarely to tell it as it is. Worse yet, since Barbara and Bill are afraid that the other will play with the truth, they each feel that their best defense is to play with it themselves. In fact, in the adversarial world where the problems that Barbara and Bill find themselves confronted with are resolved, to tell the truth is usually to be a fool, not a hero. Moreover, in such a world, Barbara and Bill will learn not what they are entitled to know but only what they can find out. In short, the law does not provide Barbara with a truth serum that will require Bill to tell her everything that he knows. Rather, the adversarial world in which the law is applied will encourage Bill to hide everything that he can, and then only to provide Barbara with a shovel to dig up whatever she can find.

In this cat-and-mouse game, Barbara is going to need help. While the help that she will receive from the court may not be sufficient, it is, nevertheless, the only help that she will get. Unfortunately, to get this help—to invoke the court's aid—it will first be necessary for her to commence litigation. Why is this so? Because, in an important sense, Bill's obligation to provide the information that Barbara wants does not exist apart from such litigation. The law, after all, does not require Bill to open his books to Barbara. It requires him to do that only in a divorce proceeding. If Barbara's lawyer is going to get the information he wants, then, and unless Bill is willing to give it to him voluntarily, he is going to have to go to court to get it. He is going to have to begin legal warfare.

And where has this brought the parties? Barbara's attorney, we will recall, has assured her that he, too, wanted to avoid litigation and to conclude a negotiated settlement. What he had neglected to tell her, however, is the Catch-22. And that is that in the adversarial world in which these negotiations take place it is almost impossible to conclude a negotiated settlement until after you have first initiated litigation.

This is not the only thing about negotiated settlements

in the adversarial world of the law that Barbara's lawyer neglected to tell her. He forgot the most important thing of all. He forgot to tell her why these settlement discussions take so long to begin, and why they get almost nowhere even when they do.

As month after month went by, and frustrated by the lack of progress, Barbara repeatedly asked her attorney why these settlement discussions had not yet been undertaken. His answer was that they were premature and that they could not properly proceed until he had first obtained all of the information he needed—until the accountants, appraisers, actuaries and other experts had completed their work. After all, it was not possible for him to conduct these discussions—to negotiate what Bill should pay her for her interest in his business—until he had first determined what that business was worth. Since he could not accept Bill's estimate of its worth, it had been necessary for him to send in an accountant of his own to make that determination. However, before he could do that, and because Barbara did not have the money necessary to pay the accountant the fee he required, it had been necessary to first make application to the court to get Bill to pay for it. And applications to the court take time. (Because they cost money, as well, Barbara's attorney had also requested an award of counsel fees for himself. Both applications were eventually granted, except that Barbara was given less than she had asked for. Since Barbara's attorney had asked for more than he expected, it was hard to tell who had won that round, though both Barbara and Bill were upset by the decision.)

When, many months later, Barbara's accountant had finally concluded his investigation, was her attorney now in a position to sit down with Bill's attorney to discuss, and hopefully to resolve, the situation? The answer, unfortunately, was no. In fact, when Barbara's accountant and Bill's accountant each concluded their extensive, and costly, examinations, they had almost nothing to talk about. This might have been the case had their attorneys agreed to hire a single, impartial accountant to review Bill's books and records so as to place a value, or at least a range of values, on his business. However, their attorneys did not do this. Rather, and just as Bill and Barbara had sought separate attorneys—not to tell them what the law was but to make a case for them—so, too, their lawyers had employed separate forensic accountants to do the same thing. And this is exacxtly what they did. Thus, Barbara's accountant concluded that Bill's business was worth approximately $600,000. Bill's accountant, on the other hand, felt that the business was worth no more than $250,000. All this time and effort had not brought them closer to an agreement, as Barbara had been led to believe it would. It had not even provided them with a framework in which to discuss one. On the contrary, it had only left them with a problem, as neither Barbara's attorney nor Bill's attorney would accept the other's evaluation, and the difference was too big to split.

What was the reaction of Barbara's attorney toward the evaluation of his accountant and Bill's accountant? Ironically, though he had very purposefully hired an accountant to present a best-case scenario as to the value of Bill's business (just as Bill had tried to make out a worst-case scenario), Barbara's attorney accepted the evaluation of his own accountant as if it were gospel, and dismissed that of Bill's accountant as an unmitigated lie. And Bill's attorney returned the compliment.

While Barbara and Bill may have been surprised by the tremendous difference in their accountants' separate evaluations, their attorneys really were not. To be sure, they may have each really believed that what they were trying to do was to come up with an accurate value. That may have been incredibly naive on their parts, but they may have believed it anyway. But that naivete did not extend to their believing that the other's motives were as pure. This being so, Barbara's and Bill's attorneys both knew that it was unlikely, at least at this stage in the proceedings, that the two of them were going to be able to sit down and negotiate a settlement. (Barbara, after all, was not going to conclude an agreement on the basis of Bill's evaluation of his business' worth when her own accountant had told her that it was worth twice that amount.) This is why, despite all of the talk of avoiding litigation, Barbara's attorney had had no reluctance in commencing it, for he knew that it was very unlikely that they would be able to resolve the matter without the court's intervention.

The much-touted procedures of discovery and disclosure, which are supposed to be both great virtues and great benefits of our adversarial system, did not serve the purpose of bringing about a negotiated settlement, as Barbara and Bill had been led to believe they would. But this, unfortunately, is not the worst of it. The worst of it is that they made the likelihood of such a settlement all the more remote. For Barbara's and Bill's attorneys employed a procedure that was destined to do more than to leave them with a problem—to leave them with two such very different estimates as to the value of Bill's business as to make a compromise, and a settlement, possible. In employing a procedure that was destined to lead to such a result, they also unwittingly increased the lack of trust between Barbara and Bill.

To be sure, Barbara had nothing to do with the evaluation of her accountant, other than to authorize it, and even this was more her attorney's doing than her own. This is not how Bill will see it, however. On the contrary, and fanning the flames of the difficult dealings that he is struggling with, he will credit Barbara as having been its author. Barbara, for her part, will do exactly the same thing when she learns the conclusion that Bill's accountant has come to. Thus, rather than decrease the likelihood of further litigation, this exercise in creative accounting has only increased it, as litigation, after all, is the only means that either Bill or Barbara can legally employ to get back at the other. And, in their anger at the injustice of the other's position, this is what each now wants to do.

Nothing for Nothing

There is something else about adversarial proceedings and the attitudes of Barbara's and Bill's lawyers that tends to promote litigation—tends to cause each of the parties to feel that they will not be able to accomplish anything without the court's intervention—and this is the fact that their attorneys seem to be unable to solve even the simplest problems that the two of them have. It is not only that their attorneys are stymied and unable to agree on a complete settlement. They cannot agree on even the smallest details.

Life, after all, must go on while Barbara's and Bill's lawyers do what it is that they do. And because life must go on, decisions must be made. For example, on April 15th, Bill will have to file his federal and state income tax returns. And since it is to his (and Barbara's) advantage to file a joint return, he will want Barbara to join with him in filing them. Nor is there anything unusual in this. On the contrary, they have filed joint income tax returns throughout their marriage. Nor did Barbara ever give very much thought to this. In fact, more likely than not, she has not even bothered to look at the returns. She has just signed them.

Her attorney, however, will give a great deal of thought to this. In fact, almost instinctively, he will be very reluctant to have Barbara sign this return. Why is this? As we have seen previously, part of the answer has to do with the question of risk. If Barbara joins with Bill in signing this return, she becomes potentially liable for any taxes that Bill may owe. Not only on the income that he reports, but on any income that he does not report as well. And on any deductions that he claims that may later be disallowed. Barbara's attorney, of course, does not know whether the income that

Bill declares on this return is accurate. In fact, he may well believe that it is not. In either case, he does not want Barbara to assume this risk. To be sure, she has done this on numerous occasions in the past. But this was before Barbara's attorney was involved in her affairs and was making the decisions in her life. This was before Barbara had a legal hound dog at her side to point out all of life's potential pitfalls and to decide what was in her best interests.

There is a less obvious, but just as troublesome, risk that will concern Barbara's attorney and cause him to decline to let Barbara join with Bill in filing a joint return as she always has done. Particularly if Bill is self-employed, but in many instances even if he is not, Barbara's attorney may not want to concede that Bill's income is as he has reported it to be to the federal government. In fact, one of the things that may be standing between the two of them and a settlement is the question of what Bill's income is— Barbara's attorney claiming it is more than he reports, to justify the demand of support and maintenance that he has made on her behalf, and Bill insisting that it is not, to justify his own position. Barbara's attorney may therefore be concerned—whether he has reason to be or not—that, if Barbara signs this return, it may later be construed to be an acknowledgement on her part that Bill's income was as he reported it.

Bill's lawyer proposes to assuage these fears, and to pave the way for Barbara to be able to sign the return, by having Bill sign a letter guaranteeing that none of this will happen. He will agree that if there are any additional taxes or penalties due on the return, he and he alone will be responsible for them. He will further agree that Barbara's joining with him in signing the return will not be deemed an admission on her part that his income is as he reported it, nor will it bar her from claiming that it is more. Now Barbara's attorney cannot object to her signing the return.

Unfortunately, there is still a problem, and it has to do with the fact that Bill (and now Barbara) will be entitled to a refund on this return. Why is this a problem? It never was in the past. It is a problem because Bill's and Barbara's attorneys are going to have very different ideas about what should happen to that refund check.

From Barbara's attorney's standpoint, Barbara should get half of that refund. In fact, if she doesn't, why should she sign the return, even if Bill is willing to give her the letter of protection that he has offered to her? Barbara did not hire her lawyer to do Bill favors. After all, what favors is Bill's lawyer doing for her? If Barbara is going to do something for Bill, there must be something in it for her. Besides, Barbara could use that money to pay for certain things that the money that Bill is giving her does not cover. In short, there is no more reason that the money should be in Bill's pocket than in hers. At least this is how it will appear to Barbara's lawyer.

Bill, of course, is going to see it very differently. In fact, he is going to view the demand of Barbara's attorney as nothing short of highway robbery. This tax refund is not a windfall, as would be the case if he had just won the lottery. It is a portion of the income that he uses to support Barbara and their children, and he was counting on it to pay certain bills that he had been unable to meet that were beginning to mount up. Barbara just wants to grab anything and everything that she can. At least this is how it will appear to Bill.

What will be the outcome? Sometimes Bill will give into Barbara's blackmail—and blackmail is what he will consider it to be. To make matters worse, from his standpoint it will now be Barbara's blackmail and not just her attorney's. Sometimes it may produce a Mexican standoff, with the problem being postponed, although not solved, by Bill filing for an extension. Whatever the outcome, however, the atmosphere will have been poisoned with further misunderstanding and distrust.

Nor will it make any difference if the question at issue is a small one, and of relatively little significance. Barbara's

and Bill's attorneys will still be unwilling or unable to resolve it. Bill has decided to move out of his and Barbara's
home and has found another place to live. However, and
since it is not furnished, he would like to have some of the
furniture in the home, including the color television and the
stereo equipment. And so he has his attorney call Barbara's
attorney to work it out.

It is a small enough matter. Nevertheless, it will present
as large an obstacle as the Rocky Mountains. To begin with,
Barbara's attorney really doesn't view Bill's problems as
being his problems. He therefore really has little interest in
solving them. To be sure, he does not want the issue to get
out of hand and to create more problems than are necessary. But aside from this, he couldn't care less.

But it is not just that he has no interest in Bill's problems or that he doesn't want to do him any favors. It is that
he doesn't want to give anything away, let alone something
for nothing. He is not presiding over a giveaway show. On
the contrary, he is trying to get as much for Barbara as he
can. And this means that he will need everything he has—
as many trading coupons as the game will provide him.
After all, suppose, as part of the final settlement, Barbara
wants to keep the china and silverware. But suppose that
Bill, operating on the same principle that you should never
give something away for nothing, objects and wants something in return. If Barbara has already let him take the color
television and the stereo equipment, what will she have left
to give him in exchange? Thus, and since she may need it
later to trade with, better not to concede it to him now.

But how does Barbara's lawyer know that Bill will object to Barbara keeping the china and silverware—or something else that she may want and ask for? He doesn't, of
course. Nevertheless, and since he certainly doesn't assume that Bill's lawyer will be willing to do Barbara any
favors or give her anything for nothing, he can't afford to
take any chances. In the legal warfare that Barbara's and
Bill's divorce has become, the safest course is to concede

nothing and to hold onto everything, for you may need it later. In a world such as this, the rule that governs the play is nothing for nothing, and it will quickly become both the watchword and Barbara's and Bill's guiding light.

Self-Help

There is one final reason that one or both of the attorneys may resort to litigation, either initially or very early on in the proceedings. As we have noted, Barbara and Bill will not be able to tread water with their lives for months or perhaps years, while their lawyers get them out of the mess that they have put them in. Rather, life will have to go on, and that means that decisions will have to be made. However, since neither Barbara nor Bill will be willing to concede almost anything at this point, it will be hard, as we have seen, for the two of them, or their attorneys, to agree on almost anything. As a result, they will each be left with no alternative other than to resort to self-help.

Sometimes what is done is done out of anger. Sometimes it is done in retaliation for something that the other has done. And sometimes it is done because Barbara or Bill honestly believes that there is no other choice. It makes no difference. If the other party takes issue or offense at the action, or believes that his position or rights have been impaired, he will seek redress. Other than by resorting to self-help himself—which he may also do—the only recourse that he has is to commence litigation and seek the aid of the court.

Let us give an example of how this occurs. Suppose that, while the negotiations between their attorneys are supposedly taking place, Bill decides to leave Barbara's and his home to establish a separate residence for himself. There is now a problem, and this is, how much money will be give to Barbara for her and their children's needs? Since the amount that Bill will voluntarily give Barbara for this purpose will be based on many considerations other than what is appropriate and what they need, one of the first things that Barbara's lawyer will do will be to seek a temporary order of the court setting the amount that Bill is required to pay to her. Whatever the court's decision will be, it will rarely aid in the resolution of the matter. In fact, it is almost destined to do just the opposite.

Why is this? Because in all likelihood, neither Barbara nor Bill will be pleased with the court's order—she will feel that she was given too little while he will feel that he was required to pay too much. As a result, and rather than reinforcing their faith in those judicial proceedings, they will each be encouraged in the belief that their ultimate success is dependent on extra-judicial means—on their resorting to further self-help. This, and the anger that the court's decision will cause each of them to direct at the other, will invariably set off a new wave of actions and reactions that will again require one or both of them to resort to the court in what will soon become an ever-escalating process.

Suppose, however, that one of the parties is, in fact, pleased with the order—Barbara feels that she got more from the court than Bill was willing to give her, or Bill feels that Barbara got less than she expected. If this is the case, the winning party will attempt to hold onto his or her victory—to protract the proceedings as long as he or she can in order to force the other to buckle under. Since the other party cannot permit this to happen, he or she will be forced either to seek further help from the court or to resort to extra-judicial means to improve his or her position. In short, the parties will find themselves committed to litigation, whether they like it or not, and no matter how earnestly their attorneys may express their commitment to negotiated, out-of-court settlements.

Getting It Right Versus Getting It Wrong

There is one final factor about adversarial legal proceedings, and the way lawyers think, that must be taken into account in order to understand why so many divorce proceedings are litigated and why the settlements that divorce lawyers boast of so often take place only on the courthouse steps. To understand this, it will be necessary to look beyond their rhetoric, which all too often is simply for public consumption, to their underlying attitudes and assumptions.

As we have already seen, one of the reasons why divorce lawyers turn so easily, and so often, to litigation, is that they do not see it as being objectionable in the sense that the general public does, or as being distinct from the negotiating process. The other reason is that, while they may profess that they would prefer a negotiated settlement, they do not see a negotiated settlement as being an end in itself. To be more accurate, while they may view a settlement as being an important goal, there are other things that they see as being more important.

One of the worst consequences of viewing divorce as being a legal event, rather than a personal event, in a couple's life—of seeing divorce as representing the proper application of legal rules, called legal rights, to the issues that a couple's divorce poses, rather than seeing these rules as being simply a means to resolve the problems incident to their divorce— has been to exaggerate the importance of these rules. Now that these rules have been elevated to rights—to ends in themselves—the primary concern is how the issues are resolved and not whether they are resolved at all. In short, divorce lawyers are much more interested in getting it right than they are in getting it done. In fact, if they cannot get it right, they would prefer not to get it done at all.

Perhaps this is merely two different ways of looking at the same thing. Unfortunately, and as all too many separating and divorcing couples can attest, seeing divorce as being primarily concerned with the proper application of legal rules has very serious implications. If one sees divorce as being primarily a personal event in a couple's life that has left them, and the members of their immediate family, in a state of crisis, then it follows, as night follows day, that they must be helped through this traumatic experience as quickly as possible. If this view is the more appropriate one, then the dichotomy between getting it right and getting it done that divorce lawyers insist upon will not hold. On the contrary, to get it right means to get it done. More importantly, to fail to get it done means, of necessity, to get it wrong.

Divorce lawyers, of course, do not see it that way. Confusing means with ends, they have made the legal rules that people employ when they cannot find better ones into objects of reverence, like the Holy Grail and the Lost Ark. And with objects of reverence, of course, there can be no compromise. Nor does one question the time, effort or financial sacrifice that may be necessary in order to obtain them.

This, then, is what belies the myth that what divorce lawyers really want is a negotiated settlement. They want a negotiated settlement, but they will accept it only on their own terms—they will accept it only if it is right. But since Barbara's and Bill's attorneys will never agree on what is right—since it is an inherent feature of our adversarial legal system that they will always view what is right from very disparate positions—the conditions for a negotiated settlement will almost never exist.

Barbara and Bill, unfortunately, will not understand this. Rather, each will believe that the reason, and only reason, why they have been unable to conclude an agreement is because of the other's unreasonableness and intrasigence. How could it be otherwise when all that they want is what they have been assured by their attorneys they are legally entitled to? This, of course, will only further reinforce the anger that they will each feel and, with it, the factors that will make a settlement between them so difficult.

In time, Barbara's and Bill's attorneys will abandon any efforts to reach a settlement at all. In fact, this much-touted goal will all but be forgotten until they are reminded, usually at the courthouse steps, that this, after all, is what it is really all about. When it is finally hammered out at the eleventh hour, their lawyers will take credit for it nevertheless. Worse yet, they will even point to it as proof of their preference for a negotiated settlement rather than litigation. But the worst irony is that, when all is said and done, they will not have gotten it right anyway. They will just have taken forever to do what they should have done months, and sometimes years, before.

THE NINTH MYTH

Adversarial Legal Proceedings Are Designed To Protect The Best Interests of Children

Divorce lawyers love to talk about the best interests of children. In fact, one of their quaint conceits is that they are very interested in what happens to the children of separating and divorcing couples and that a great virtue of our adversarial legal system is that it will protect their best interests. In fact, this too has become so much a part of legal mythology that we no longer question it. Question it we must, however, because it is not so. On the contrary, nothing could be farther from the truth.

Since one could write a book about the very damaging effects of adversarial divorce proceedings upon children—and many books have been written on just this subject—we will limit our focus to one issue alone. This is the issue of their children's best interests when Barbara and Bill are not able to agree as to their custody, and when the matter has to be resolved by a court of law.

There will be three principal players in this drama: the lawyers who will argue the case, the judge who will decide it and the mental health professionals who will give their considered opinions. Let us begin with Barbara's and Bill's attorneys. Are they interested in the best interests of their children? The answer, unfortunately, is not very flattering. As we have seen, a lawyer's job is not to get what is fair for his client. It is to get what is best for him. And what is best for him is to get as much as he can, whether this is fair or not. What is best for Barbara and Bill here? It is to win the case and to get custody of their children, regardless of whether or not this is in their children's best interests.

But surely Barbara's and Bill's lawyers have an obligation to their children as well? Surely they are concerned with what is best for them? Don't be so sure about it, for it isn't so. A lawyers's obligation is to his client. For it is his client, after all, who will pay his fee. And Barbara's and Bill's children are not their lawyers' clients. It is Barbara and Bill who are. In fact, it might well be a dereliction of Barbara's and Bill's attorneys' obligations to them were they to concern themselves with whether the desired result will be best for their children.

Certainly there must be something wrong here. Certainly the paramount concern of Barbara's and Bill's attorneys to vouchsafe what is in the best interests of their children could not possibly be subordinate to Barbara's and Bill's own desires to win custody of them. Nor could their attorneys' obligations possibly be compromised by the fact that it is Barbara and Bill who will pay their fees. Nevertheless, this is the concern expressed by Richard E. Crouch, a well-known and respected matrimonial lawyer. And if one is tempted to dismiss this as the opinion, if not the misguided aberration, of but one matrimonial lawyer, it should be pointed out that this one matrimonial lawyer was, at the time that he made that statement, Chairman of the Ethical Practices and Procedures Committee of the Family Law Section of the American Bar Association. No, if our adversarial system is concerned with protecting Barbara's and Bill's children, we will have to look elsewhere than to their lawyers for that protection.

Let us turn then to the judge who will determine the matter. To be sure, he is truly interested in the best interests of Barbara's and Bill's children. Nevertheless, there are still some problems. To begin with, and although his black robes may be designed to hide many things, the one thing that they cannot hide is the fact that there is nothing in either his background or his professional training that would enable him to decide, let alone to know, what is in Barbara's and Bill's children's best interests. In short, while the state may have invested him with the power to make that determination, the one thing that grant of authority was not capable of doing was to give him the wisdom that was needed to properly make it.

But isn't that what our legal system is designed to accomplish—to provide the judge with that ability? It may be designed for that purpose, but, and as is so often the case with out adversarial legal system, it works far better in principle than it does in practice. While there are a number of factors that account for this—that the setting employed is not the most conducive for a proper determination of the question; that the judge is constrained by certain principles of law and evidence that reflect the administration of a judicial system and even political considerations far more than they do the best interests of Barbara's and Bill's children—we will limit ourselves to but one. And this is the fact that the protagonists in the drama, Barbara's and Bill's respective lawyers, will conduct the proceeding in such a way as to make any rational inquiry almost impossible.

Very few custody disputes involve choices between black and white—between a father who is an eagle scout and a mother who is a drug-addicted prostitute. If they were, they would be very easy to decide. Nor would it take the wisdom of Solomon to decide them. Rather, they involve choices between two people who, as Barbara and Bill, are basically decent human beings. To be sure, they have different styles and even different nurturing abilities. But they are both adequate parents and the children's needs would not be ill served by being in either of their care and custody.

Given this fact, neither Barbara's attorney nor Bill's attorney will attempt to demonstrate that it is in their children's best interest that custody be awarded to their client. (Since it is impossible to know how their children will fare over the next ten years were they to be in Barbara's care or Bill's care, let alone to make a comparison—one would need a crystal ball to know or do that—it is simply not possible to demonstrate this.) Rather, their argument will be that it is not in their best interests that their custody be awarded to the other party. In short, and lacking any meaningful criteria, let alone understanding, as to what these children's best interests are, the attempt will be made simply to disqualify the other party as a fit custodian—to make him the bad guy.

What started out as a supposed inquiry in aid of the best interests of these children will thus quickly turn into something that is anything but that. In fact, when Barbara's and Bill's lawyers get through, it will be nothing short of a travesty. The most casual occurrences will be taken out of context and exaggerated in the reporting in each of the parties' lawyers' attempts to discredit the other. Was it Barbara's habit to have an occasional glass of wine with one of her girlfriends in the late afternoon? Then she will be made out to be an alcoholic. Had Bill, on one occasion, slapped one of the children as a punishment? Then he will be made out to be a child abuser. Was it Barbara's habit occasionally to leave the children with a babysitter when she spent the evening out with some of her girlfriends? Then she will be made out to be a neglectful parent. Had Bill been guilty of the casual use of marijuana on a few occasions? Then he will be made out to be a drug abuser. Had Barbara ever lost her temper and used less-than-befitting language to her children? Then she will be made out to be an irresponsible mother. Did Bill spend long hours away from his family, devoted to his work? Then he will be made out to be a workaholic and a less-than-interested parent. And, worst of all, had Barbara been emotionally (sexually) involved outside of the marriage? Then she will be made out to be immoral, and a bad influence on her children, and clearly unfit to be their custodian.

And what of Barbara's and Bill's children in all of this? What role will they play in this barrage of charges and countercharges? If it is their best interests that are supposedly at issue, then surely they should be heard from. We will never know the full extent of the damage done to children who have been made unwitting participants in this disgraceful charade—not only in being brought forward to be corroborating witnesses to their parents' supposed misconduct but, and worse, in being asked to decide between them. If both of your parents were drowning and you had only one life preserver to throw to them, to whom would you throw it? A wonderful question to ask Barbara's and Bill's children, all in the name of guaranteeing their best interests.

Let us turn now to the last performer in this demi-drama—the mental health professionals who will be asked to give their considered opinion and expert testimony in these proceedings. It is fair to say that any mental health professional who has any familiarity with custody disputes, particularly those settled by courts of law in adversarial legal proceedings, would accept the following conclusions:

1. The procedure that the law will employ to make a decision as to the custody of Barbara's and Bill's children will be more damagng to them than any possible decision that the court could make, even one it could make by flipping a coin. And this is not only true in Barbara's and Bill's case, it is true in the vast majority of instances.

2. Although the dispute between Barbara and Bill may be over their children, in actual fact it has little, if anything, to do with them. On the contrary—and this, too, is true in the vast majority of instances—what is really happening here is that one of them is playing out their anger at the other by engaging in a tug of war over their children. Moreover, their anger is so overwhelming, and their desire to get back and to get even so great, that they are even willing to pull their own children apart in the process if that is what it will take.

3. What is truly in the best interest of Barbara's and Bill's children is not to have a court decide the dispute

between their parents, but to resolve it and thereby hopefully to end it.

4. Except where either Barbara or Bill is guilty of having breached minimal societal standards, it is never in their children's best interests that the decisions in their lives be made by courts of law or other outside agencies. Rather, it is in their best interest that the conduct and control of their lives be left in the hands of their parents. Accordingly, if Barbara and Bill have lost the ability to make those decisions, our efforts should be directed at restoring that ability to them, not at delegating the responsibility to others.

If this is so, how is it that mental health professionals have become such unwitting allies in a process that, by definition, ignores and then violates every one of these principles? And how is it that they have been blinded to the terrible damage this does to everyone concerned, and most particularly to the children who are caught in the middle?

The answer is that they have been taken in by abstractions and by the same legal mythology that Barbara and Bill have bought. In short, they have had their eye taken off the mark by all of the talk about the best interests of Barbara's and Bill's children. And because they have had their eye taken off the mark, they have willingly agreed to participate in a process that has nothing to do with Barbara's and Bill's children's best interests, and will do anything but serve them.

But aren't these mental health professionals the experts here, and don't they really know what is in Barbara's and Bill's children's best interests? The answer is no—Barbara and Bill are the experts and the only ones who should properly decide what is best for their children. Thus, if Barbara and Bill have lost the ability to exercise their expertise, then the best thing for their children would be to restore that ability to them, not to assign the job to someone else who, by definition, will simply give his opinion, and then walk away and wash his hands of the whole affair. After all, it is Barbara and Bill, not their lawyers, their paid experts or even the judge for that matter, who will be required to raise their children and make the important decisions in their lives when the matter is concluded and all of the other performers in the drama have left the stage.

Even if these mental health professionals are truly the experts they claim to be, however, there is still another, even more serious, problem. As we have seen, adversarial lawyers will not provide the court (the judge) with impartial evidence that will aid it in its determination. On the contrary, they will provide the court with conflicting testimony that will only cloud the issue and make its determination all the more difficult. Thus, the mental health professionals who will give testimony on Barbara's and Bill's behalf will not step forward as friends of the court. They will not even step forward as friends of Barbara's and Bill's children. They will appear as paid experts—as hired guns—on behalf of Barbara and Bill. Nor will Barbara's or Bill's lawyers call them as witnesses, or pay them for their services, until they have first assured themselves that they will shoot in the desired direction. Needless to say, and unless Bill is an eagle scout and Barbara a drug-addicted prostitute, neither of their lawyers will have any difficulty finding a mental health professional who will shoot in any direction they want.

Will Barbara's and Bill's lawyers really stoop this low? Could they possibly have so little concern over what will happen to their children in all of this? There is, of course, a way to test this out. If Barbara's and Bill's lawyers are truly interested in the well-being of their children, as they insist they are, there is one thing that they could do that would truly be in their best interests. That would be to enter into an agreement that Barbara and Bill will seek the opinion of only one mental health professional and that they will be bound by that opinion. They could thereby not only decide the question but, and just as importantly, they

could get that decision quickly and without having to subject Barbara's and Bill's children, or even themselves for
that matter, to a contested custody trial.

There is an even better way to test this out. They could
refer Barbara and Bill to a divorce mediator would help
them address the very difficult feelings that one of them is
experiencing, and that have fueled their custody dispute, in
the hope that the two of them would be able to resolve it
and to end it, rather than to decide it. That truly would be
in the best interests of Barbara's and Bill's children.

Will Barbara's or Bill's lawyers agree to either of these
proposals? It would be a very serious mistake to bet on it.
It well may be that they are both interested in the well-
being of Barbara's and Bill's children. But they are only
interested in their well-being if there is nothing else that
they are more interested in. And as we have seen, what
they are more interested in is the best interests of Barbara
and Bill.

Thus, neither Barbara's lawyer nor Bill's lawyer is very
likely to agree to the first proposal. Why is this? Because
neither of them has any control over the impartial mental
health professional who will be chosen for the job. And
because they do not have any control over him, they do not
know what he might say or what his opinion might be. He
might even come to the conclusion that custody should be
given, not to their client, but to the other party. And this
will not do. After all, Barbara's and Bill's attorneys were
each hired to get custody for their own client, not to give
it away to the other's client.

What about the second suggestion? Certainly there is
not the same danger here. After all, if Barbara and Bill are
able, through the mediator's efforts, to resolve the issue of
the custody of their children, then they will both have had
to agree to it. If this is so, there is no danger, as is admittedly the case with the first suggestion, that either of them
will be left with an agreement that was imposed upon them.

Nevertheless, neither Barbara's nor Bill's attorney is

likely to recommend this on their own. In fact, there is a good chance that they will discourage Barbara and Bill from considering it even if they were to suggest it themselves. (Barbara's lawyer will try to dissuade her by telling her that she will be no match for Bill if he is not there by her side. Bill's lawyer, on the other hand, will try to dissuade him by telling him that there is a very real danger that the mediator may side with Barbara because she is a woman.)

Why will they do this and what do they really have to fear? What they have to fear—and for very good reason—is that the mediator will very quickly resolve the issue. But what is the danger in this? The danger is that if Barbara and Bill see how quickly and easily the mediator disposed of the Third World War that their dispute over the custody of their children had become, they might decide to stick around and let the mediator help them resolve the smaller wars that are raging and standing between them and an agreement. That, however, will not do, for now we are talking, not about what is best for Barbara and Bill and their children but, about what is best for their attorneys. And their interests, after all, are the most important of all.

The idea that divorce lawyers are concerned with the best interests of children, or that our adversaral legal system is the one best designated to protect their interests, is thus only another of the many fables in legal mythology. Just the opposite is the case. In fact, if we wanted to design a system that would truly serve the best interests of children, and if, at every stage of the construction, we did exactly the opposite of what made sense and what was truly in their best interests, when we got through, and with a little bit of luck, what we would be left with would be our adversarial legal system.

THE TENTH MYTH

The Use of Adversarial Legal Proceedings
Represents a Sensible Way
For Divorcing Couples to Solve Their Problems

It is a truism that lawyers are not held in very high regard in our society. To be sure, lawyers may flatter themselves in the belief that what they are doing is promoting the common good, and divorce lawyers probably flatter themselves with this conceit more than most. Nevertheless, there will be few amongst us who believe this. In fact, it is hard to imagine a group, let alone a profession, that is held in lower esteem. The incredible number of lawyer jokes bear adequate witness to this.

If this is so, why is it that so many couples turn, almost instinctively, to the law and to adversarial legal proceedings at the very first thought of divorce? Why, when they know what is in store for them, do they literally place their lives in the hands of lawyers? They do not do this because they think that lawyers know what is best for them, because they do not really believe this. Nor do they do it because they think that lawyers will be able to provide them with easy answers to their problems. Whatever one may believe about lawyers and the law, it is not that they act swiftly or that their services come cheaply. No, if they turn to lawyers, and subject themselves to the terrible cost that will inevitably be involved, they do it for an entirely different reason. They do it out of fear. But what is it that they are afraid of? They are afraid that they will not have enough. They are afraid that they will be left with less than what they need.

For most married couples, there was just enough, and sometimes just barely enough, to go around when they lived together. Now, and with one swift blow, all of this has changed. It is as if Barbara and Bill have a tablecloth that used to fit, or at least barely fit, their kitchen or dining room table. The table represents the problem and the tablecloth represents the resources (the money) that they have to meet it. The problem has now gotten bigger, however, because they have just gotten a new, bigger table. Thus, where there used to be one rent to pay or one household to support, there will now be two. Where, previously, there was one telephone bill that had to be paid at the beginning of the month, there will now be two. And so it goes, right down the line.

Barbara's and Bill's problem may have gotten bigger, but their resources, unfortunately, have not. Thus, they may have just acquired a new, larger table, but they have been left with the same, old tablecloth. And it is just not going to cover their new table. It is too small, and this is the problem.

But this is not the first time that Barbara and Bill have had financial problems—that there was not enough money to go around—not enough money to cover all of their expenses. However, they did not run off to lawyers for help then. Nor would it have ever occurred to them to do so. After all, lawyers had no special knowledge, let alone a magic wand, that would have filled their pockets and thereby solved their problems. If this is so, what makes them believe that they will be able to perform this magical feat now? The answer, of course, is that they really don't. It is just that they are each so afraid that they will not be left with enough that their fear overwhelms their common sense. This is particularly true in Barbara's case, since she is economically dependent upon the support that she will receive from Bill.

Fear may be what initially gives birth to Barbara's and Bill's anxieties, but there is something else that will fuel them. In the past, if the two of them had a problem, it was their common problem. There may not have been enough to go around, and they may not have known where what was needed would come from. Nevertheless, they at least had the security of knowing that they were in it together, and that fact tended to contain their fears and to prevent them from becoming overwhelmed. Now, however, and in but a moment of time, this security has been shattered. They no longer feel that they are in it together. Rather, each of them feels that they have been left all alone. Again, this will be especially true of Barbara.

Thus, Barbara and Bill will not turn to lawyers because they believe that the rules of law that lawyers apply are better than the personal considerations that they might themselves employ. Nor will they turn to them because they believe that the application of these rules will leave them with more. How could they when they do not even know what these rules are, let alone whether they will help them or hurt them? They will run off to lawyers simply because they are afraid. Barbara will run off to a lawyer because she is afraid that Bill will not give her all that she needs. But what is Bill afraid of? He is afraid that Barbara will ask for more than he can afford, and that what he will be left with will therefore not be enough. And so he will run off to a lawyer as well.

How are Barbara's and Bill's lawyers going to solve their problem? More importantly, how are they going to see to it that Barbara and Bill will each be left with all they feel that they need? The answer, of course, is that they will not. As we have seen, the mythology that sends separating and divorcing couples off to lawyers and to lawyer-land is a fairy tale that only a child or a fool would believe. Barbara's and Bill's lawyers do not have any special power that will enable them to solve their problem—to increase the size of the tablecloth so that it will fit their new table. Worse yet, neither of them even considers that this is what they have been hired to do. After all, lawyers have not been trained to solve problems. They have been trained to make cases.

If this is so, what, then, will they do? What they will do—what divorce lawyers always do—is engage in a very unseemly, and just as costly, tug of war over the tablecloth. Since there is not enough to go around, and since neither Barbara's lawyer nor Bill's lawyer has any desire to solve the problem for the other, they will each advise their clients that the object of the game is simply to get as much as they can, and to give as little as they have to. Moreover, if Barbara or Bill should inquire what the rules of the game are, they will be told that there are no rules, that it is each man for himself, and that it is anything that the law will allow. And, as Barbara and Bill will both quickly learn, the law will allow a great deal.

The War of the Roses

Fairy tales may be amusing and proper reading material for children. But even with children, flights from reality are not to be encouraged beyond a certain point. Thus, when adults take them too literally, there is usually a price to be paid. In the case of separating and divorcing couples who buy legal mythology, this price is very heavy indeed.

As we all know, modern divorce has come to resemble the War of the Roses that took place in England between the houses of York and Lanchaster in the fifteenth century. In fact, and as a recent popular movie of that name graphically documented, it has become a form of legal warfare. To be sure, the conduct of the protagonists in that film was somewhat exaggerated, but critics who dismissed it on that account did so at the expense of an important point. As outrageous as the conduct of separating and divorcing couples typically is to one another, and even to their children, it has, unfortunately, become accepted as being both an inherent and an inevitable part of the divorcing process.

Thus, it was not possible for the film to portray what has become standard practice in divorce, as it is so commonplace that we have lost the ability to see it as being as inappropriate and irresponsible, and at times even as irrational, as it is. Rather, if there was any hope that we would be able to see it as being the institutionalized insanity that it has become, it was necessary to carry it to its logical extreme.

And that, of course, was the point. If we laughed or were even offended by what was being portrayed, it was not because it was out of character. The protagonists in the film may have gone further than we would have liked, and even further than we would have expected. But their conduct, as extreme as it was, was not out of character. On the contrary, it was of a piece with what we have come to expect and what we therefore routinely accept.

There was one thing that was not exaggerated, however, and that was how the protagonists felt, and the strong—and at times overpowering—emotions that possessed both of them. This, too, has become the accepted norm in divorce to the point where we no longer question it. For we all know that, by whatever name it is called, modern divorce has become the War of the Roses.

While the legal profession may encourage this belief, and then condone the legal insanity that lawyers routinely subject each of the parties to by saying that, even if it is not a particularly attractive spectacle, it is, nevertheless, inevitable, there were those who began to have some second thoughts. Beginning in the late 1970s, and particularly in the early 1980s, those who dealt with separating and divorcing couples, and those who were charged with the responsibility of picking up the pieces of broken and shattered families when lawyers got through with them, began to question the legal mythology that caused husbands and wives to run off and employ a process that they knew hadn't worked effectively for others and wouldn't work any better for them. What was it that caused them to turn their lives over to lawyers when they knew that they would only make things worse, not better?

Those who asked these questions came to a very disturbing conclusion. Separating and divorcing couples turned to lawyers, and to the unseemly legal tug of war that they engaged in, because legal mythology reinforced their fears. To be sure, separating and divorcing couples were faced with a serious life problem that the two of them would have to address. But why were they so afraid that it would be such a life-and-death, no-holds-barred, struggle that they felt compelled to immediately run off and hire legal gladiators? Because legal mythology had convinced them that this was exactly what it would be.

Divorce lawyers had gone and made a circus of divorce and had then persuaded separating and divorcing couples that, because it was a circus, they had to go out and employ clowns and a ringmaster to organize and run the spectacle. And when divorcing couples complained that the clowns and ringmaster were not really funny, and that they came at too high a price, legal mythology then only further reinforced their fears by telling them that if they did not pay the piper for his mad tune, the performance they would find themselves watching might not be a circus. It might be a tragedy. In fact, it might be their own funeral.

Context

Those who began to take exception to the message being sent out by our adversarial legal system that divorce was war and that there could only be one winner—that it was only possible for Barbara or Bill to solve their problem at the expense of the other—and who began to question the legal mythology that supported it, came to another disturbing conclusion. And that was that it was actually the supposed benefits of our adversarial legal system that were, in fact, its worst drawback and that created the problem for

Barbara and Bill. Mediators coined a phrase to express this. It was called context.

To illustrate this, let us consider one of the legal profession's most sacred cows: confidentiality. If a divorce lawyer were to be asked what he thought was one of the most important benefits of our adversarial legal system, invariably he would answer that it was the fact that what took place between Barbara and Bill and their respective attorneys was confidential. Just as Barbara and Bill are free to talk to their physicians, their therapists and their clergymen secure in the knowledge that what takes place between them will be held in the strictest confidence, so, too, they may rely upon the same assurance when they confide in their attorneys. That, so it will be claimed, is one of the great virtues of our legal system. In fact, that is why divorce lawyers claim it is superior to mediation, for one of the drawbacks of mediation, so it will again be claimed, is that confidentiality does not exist in the discussions that take place between the couple and their mediator.

Legal mythology notwithstanding, it is not so. Confidentiality is not one of the great virtues of our adversarial legal system. It is one of its most serious defects.

Why is confidentiality so important to Bill's lawyer? For that matter, what is it that he is so anxious to keep confidential? What he wants to keep confidential—what he wants to hide from Barbara, from the court and from the world—is the truth. Bill is in business for himself, and there has been cash income that has gone unreported. When Bill talks about this cash income, his lawyer does not want Barbara or her lawyer to be present to learn about it. And he certainly doesn't want to be obligated to have to disclose it to them, or even to the court for that matter. The same is true when Bill tells him what the real value of his business is, or of other property that he may have. No, his lawyer wants to keep all of this secret—he wants to hide behind the shield of confidentiality that protects him from having to disclose the truth. Ironically, Barbara's lawyer wants to hide behind it also. Thus, when Barbara confides to him that she is really capable of working outside of the home and has, in fact, been offered employment, he does not want Bill to know this.

This raises a problem. Our modern divorce laws uniformly require that there be full disclosure between husbands and wives as to their income and assets and as to anything else that may be relevant for a proper determination of the issues. In fact, divorce lawyers, who forever boast that this, too, is one of the great benefits of our adversarial legal system, have given a name to this. It is called disclosure and discovery. Bill is obligated to disclose the truth and Barbara has the right to discover it.

But if Barbara and Bill are each entitled to know the truth about the other's financial circumstances—if this is one of their legal rights—why do their lawyers feel that it is both appropriate and necessary that they be able to hide that truth behind the shield of confidentiality? To put it another way, why shouldn't Barbara and Bill each be present when the other tells the truth to his or her attorney? Because even though both Barbara's and Bill's lawyers would each like to know the truth about the other, neither of them wants to have to reveal the truth about themselves. Moreover, if they are forced to choose between knowing the truth or being able to hide it, they will always choose having the right to hide it. How will they justify this? By beating the drum of confidentiality until it deafens all opposition.

Disclosure and discovery, then, are not great virtues of our adversarial system of law. Rather, and given the fact that divorce lawyers invoke the doctrine of confidentiality to hide the truth, they are its necessities. Barbara and Bill will not be encouraged by their lawyers to be honest, even though that is what they were brought up to be. On the contrary, they will be made to feel that to be honest and to tell the truth is to be a fool. Thus, in the legal game of hide-and-seek and catch-me-if-you-can that lawyers play, they will each be encouraged to dig deep holes to hide their valuables. This is why disclosure and discovery are so necessary, for having encouraged them to bury the truth, the law has now made it necessary to provide each of them with a shovel to uncover it.

Nor will the shovel that Barbara and Bill each will be given be as effective a tool as lawyers pretend it is. After all, the world is a very big place in which to hide things, and it is therefore a lot easier to secret them away than it is to find them. Moreover, even if Barbara and Bill are able to unearth a great deal, they will always be afraid that they have not found all that there was to find. And they will be right.

This creates a problem. If Barbara believes that Bill will not be honest, why, then, should she be? Worse yet, if she believes that he will play with the truth, what alternative does she have but to play with it herself? And so she will. The very nature of adversarial divorce proceedings is such that it places a premium on deception and penalizes honesty. Moreover, the entire tone is one of exaggeration. Thus, the wonderful treasure hunt that lawyers organize, that they call disclosure and discovery, will not make either Barbara or Bill feel secure. On the contrary, it will only make them feel anxious.

If the context in which adversarial divorce proceedings takes place is so counterproductive, what is it about the context in which mediation takes place that will make it so much easier for Barbara and Bill to work out their problems? Again, mediators have coined a term to express this. They call it "hands on top of the table."

As we have seen, divorce lawyers meet with their clients, and plan with their clients, secretly and privately, behind closed doors. This setting in which adversarial proceedings take place—where the parties deal with one another with their hands under the table—is not one of the virtues of our adversarial legal system, as lawyers would have it. Rather, and understood from the standpoint of context, it is one of its most serious drawbacks, for the fact that one of the parties has been excluded from this meeting reinforces the very fear that is the problem in the first place.

Just the opposite is the case in divorce mediation. Here, everything takes place openly and in full view. As a result, neither Barbara nor Bill will have to worry whether certain things have taken place behind their backs. It is not going to happen, so there will be no need for them to worry. More importantly, they are meeting with their mediator to work out an amicable settlement, not to prepare for legal warfare. Thus, they will not be encouraged to plot and plan, or to lie and hide. Nor will they be made to feel that they have to. On the contrary, the message that the mediator will send out to them is that the success of their entire enterprise depends upon honesty, not upon dishonesty.

Getting legal information in mediation also tends to promote an agreement between the parties for another reason. Unlike adversarial lawyers, a mediator (and the advisory attorney who will assist the couple during the course of the mediation) will not talk out of both sides of his mouth, saying one thing to Barbara and another to Bill. Rather, and since he will answer their questions only when both of them are there, they each hear the same thing. Getting legal information in mediation is therefore not the occasion for promoting conflict between the two of them, as it is in an adversarial setting. It is the means of providing Barbara and Bill with the information they will need in order to conclude an agreement between themselves successfully.

Why does the information that Barbara and Bill receive in mediation promote an agreement when it only serves to act as a divisive factor in adversarial proceedings? Because legal rules are not used as weapons in mediation. As we have seen, legal rules are simply the advantage and disadvantage cards that Barbara's and Bill's lawyers will employ in their effort to get as much as they can and to give as little as they have to. And, as we have also seen, they will be used by their lawyers with little thought, and just as little regard, as to whether employing them in the game of legal chess that they will play will promote or impede Barbara's and Bill's ability to conclude an agreement. Quite obviously, this is not how legal rules are used in mediation. Rather, they are used either to impart information that will help Barbara and Bill make informed, intelligent decisions or to effectuate an agreement when they are having difficulty concluding one on their own.

In many instances, there is technical information that Barbara and Bill will need in order to make a decision. For example, if they own a home, there will be tax implications that have to be taken into account, no matter what decision they come to with respect to its disposition. It will therefore be the mediator's obligation to make sure that they have this information. (If the mediator is not an attorney, then the advisory attorney who will also work with them throughout the mediation will provide them with this information.)

In other instances, the mediator will employ the rules that courts apply for another purpose. At times, there may be a disagreement that is standing between Barbara and Bill and an agreement. Bill does not feel that he should have to share his retirement benefits with Barbara. From his standpoint, these are benefits that he was going to share with her, as his wife, not benefits that she had the right to take away with her after she decided to divorce him. In fact, for her to be able to leave him and to take these benefits with her is, at least as far as Bill is concerned, only to add insult to injury. From Barbara's standpoint, however, she has earned these benefits. Nor should she be penalized for her decision to divorce Bill by being forced to forego a share in them, particularly when she feels that she has made that decision for very good reasons. In short, as she would not expect Bill to give her a larger share of these benefits if the decision to divorce had been his, so, too, she does not see why she should receive a smaller share because the decision was hers.

For better or worse, and as overwhelmed with their loss

and anger as Barbara or Bill may be, divorce is not the occasion to have long, philosophical discussions, going nowhere, as to what is ultimately fair or unfair in the world. Divorce lawyers, of course, may wish to encourage the mythology that it is, and then add insult to injury by flattering themselves that, because they are lawyers, they have some special knowledge about these matters that is denied to the rest of us. But this is not its purpose. Nor are lawyers better qualified than we are to say what is fair or unfair—certainly not about our lives. The purpose of divorce is to help Barbara and Bill to put that pain and hurt behind them and get on with the business of their lives.

If they are unable to do this—if they are unable to answer the question whether Barbara should or should not receive a portion of Bill's retirement benefits—it is going to be decided for them by a court of law. If this is the case, then it might make some sense for them to know how a court views retirement benefits. Not because the rules that a court will apply— the rules that determine whether or not those benefits are marital property that the court has the power to distribute— represent what is necessarily fair or right, but because they represent the reality that Barbara and Bill are going to be confronted with if they are unable to conclude an agreement on their own, without the court's intervention. The court will not say that Barbara is making a mistake, let alone that she is breaking any law, if she decides not to ask to share in Bill's retirement benefits. But it will say that she has a right to a portion of those benefits if she wants them. If that is the case, what sense does it make for Bill to break up an agreement because he is unwilling to share them with her, when a court is only going to make him do that anyway. Far better that he be confronted with that reality without having to pay the price that getting that answer from a court will cost. More importantly, far better that Bill be confronted with that reality in a setting that will not only give him that information but, if it is, in fact, the reality that he will have to face, one that will enable him to accept it.

To be sure, if Bill were to ask that same question in an adversarial setting, his attorney might give him false levels of expectations or, and even worse, simply tell him what he wanted to hear. But, and as we have seen, that will not be doing Bill any favor. All that it will do is commit him to costly and pointless litigation. Worse yet, it will only tend to guarantee that, when he does finally learn the unpleasant truth, he will be left feeling that a terrible injustice has been done, which will make it all the more difficult for him to accept.

There is one other feature about the context in which divorce mediation takes place that is critical and that makes it so effective. Whereas adversarial legal proceedings, and divorce lawyers who are its champions, justify themselves by sending out the message that there will not be enough to go around, and that it is therefore each man for himself, divorce mediation sends out a very different message. This message is that it is not possible for either Barbara or Bill to solve their problem for themselves alone, for it is a common problem. Thus, unless they are able to conclude an agreement that they both feel they can live with, it will be of no value to either of them.

Legal mythology, of course, will tell Barbara and Bill a very different story. It will encourage each of them to believe that if they turn to adversarial proceedings, and particularly if they get themselves "good" lawyers—which is usually translated to mean tough lawyers—they will be guaranteed that they will be left with the lion's share of the tablecloth. Worse yet, and while not necessarily saying this in so many words, it will also send out the message that it should not make any difference to either of them how little the other will be left with, let alone whether they will have enough. This, of course, is worse than legal nonsense. It is legal irresponsibility.

Let us suppose, for example, that Barbara is able to find an attorney who is clever enough—or who has whatever else it takes—to get most of the tablecloth for her, leaving Bill wanting. Won't he have served her well, as he was supposed to do? Legal mythology notwithstanding, the answer is no; for when he gets through, what Barbara thought was the end of the game, and her victory, will turn out only to be the end of round one. After all, what does Barbara think that Bill will do if he is left with an agreement that he feels he cannot live with?

Divorce mediators, of course, do not traffic in legal mythology. Nor do they encourage people to believe in legal nonsense. They know that unless the agreement works for both Barbara and Bill, it will be of no use to either of them. And because they know this, this will be the message that they will send out to them. To be sure, a mediator knows that he cannot expect Barbara and Bill to see their problem in the same way. Looking at it from different angles, they will not even see the table in the same way. But this does not mean that it is not a common table. It just means that their different points of view will make it appear differently.

The context in which mediation takes place will do something else that is very important. It will help Barbara and Bill to separate the practical problems that they are faced with from the very difficult feelings that all too often overwhelm them. As we have seen, our adversarial legal system, and the legal mythology that justifies it, is totally oblivious to the fact that it only adds further fuel to these feelings, thereby making Barbara's and Bill's efforts to conclude an agreement all the more difficult.

Divorce mediation, which was born of an understanding of the very destructive power of these feelings, and the very high price that separating and divorcing couples pay in being encouraged to give expression to them, attempts just the opposite. While not questioning the validity of how either Barbara or Bill feels—since the mediator did not lead either of their lives, it would be inappropriate for him to make judgments in them—he can, nevertheless, help them understand that they can only get lost in these feelings. These feelings serve no useful purpose. Rather, they only tie them to the past and to the hurt that is associated with it. The mediator will try to help them to understand this, and to understand, as well, that if they are to look forward, they must learn to let go of them. Most importantly, he will try to help them to see that, by getting in the way of an agreement between the two of them, those feelings are preventing them from doing this.

The context in which mediation takes place promotes this in still another way. By persuading Barbara and Bill that what they have is a legal problem, legal mythology encourages them to believe that, since they are not lawyers, they are not the experts. Rather, it is their lawyers who are. In short, by buying legal mythology, Barbara and Bill also will have disenfranchised themselves. To be sure, it is their lives. Nevertheless, they are no longer the ones who are qualified to make the decisions in them. Since it is a legal problem, it is their lawyers who are now qualified.

Divorce mediation sends out a very different message. If Barbara and Bill are not the experts here, who is? Certainly not their lawyers. After all, how could their lawyers possibly know what is best for them? The answer is that they don't. In fact, and as we have seen, their lawyers have a very narrow, and therefore very distorted, view of what is best for them. Without question, the only responsible advice that Barbara and Bill can be given is that which will help them come to terms with what has happened to them, as painful as it is and as difficult as it may be for them to understand it. This is not the message that their divorce lawyers will sent out to them, however. Rather, and joining with them in their belief that each has been victimized by the other, they will then encourage them that there is some important principle that must be vindicated, and send them off on a crusade to do pointless legal battle with one another, only to come back bloody and bruised and, sometimes, scarred for life.

THE ELEVENTH MYTH

Adversarial Proceedings May Not be Perfect
But There Is No Better Way

If our adversarial legal system is such a poor instrument
for resolving the problems that people in society find themselves confronted with and if it does the terrible damage
that it does, how, then, do lawyers defend it? In very much
the same way that Winston Churchill defended democracy:
It may not be a perfect system, but it is the best that we
have so far been able to devise.

This raises a question. If our adversarial legal system
really is the best means available, why is it that the leaders
of corporate America and the representatives of organized
labor almost never employ it? And why do they turn, instead, to mediation? There are a number of reasons for this.
Moreover, they are equally sound when it comes to the
disputes that separating and divorcing couples find themselves confronted with.

What, after all, is it about the disputes between labor
and management that make them different from those between other members of society? It is that those disputes
take place within the context of an ongoing relationship?
Labor and management have worked together for years in
the past. Similarly, they are going to have to work together
in the future. Thus, and while their present dispute may
temporarily occupy center stage, it has to be understood
and resolved in keeping with the reality that the two of
them will have to go back into the factory together, and
work together, once it is settled. Nor will it do, in terms of

that ongoing relationship, for their dispute to be resolved with one of them coming out a winner and the other a loser.

The same is true with separating and divorcing couples. In most instances, their relationship has been a long one. More importantly, and where there are children, which is usually the case, it is going to be an ongoing one. Quite obviously, they have gotten to this point because, at least for one of them, it has been difficult for him or her to do business with the other, just as it has been difficult, within the context of their relationship, for that person to satisfy what he or she considers to be his or her essential needs. This, and the resultant hurt and misunderstanding, has made communication between them difficult, and at times impossible. As a result, they do not wish to be condemned to have to do more business with one another than is necessary. Nevertheless, and at least for the sake of their children, they want to be left able to do the necessary business that they must.

As experience has shown, resorting to litigation and to adversarial legal proceedings is not going to help Barbara and Bill accomplish this. On the contrary, these proceedings seem, almost by design, to insure just the opposite. Rather than encouraging any real communication between the two of them, the discussions will normally take place between their attorneys alone. Even when they do participate in those discussions, however, it will usually be only as observers—bit players consigned to the wings of the stage. Moreover, and rather than lending themselves to any form of compromise, their attorneys will commence discussions that will be formal in nature and invariably will proceed from fixed positions from which there is little, if any, departure. Worse yet, and since their demands are couched in terms of rights and obligations, and are justified on the basis of equity and fairness, they feed into the desire of one, and sometimes both, of them to look to those discussions, and to the resultant settlement, for personal vindication.

As we have seen, the climate of those proceedings, and the discussions that they encourage, is such that Barbara and Bill will be sent off with false levels of expectation that will then invariably be followed by equivalent levels of disappointment. The result is that all too often the hurt associated with their divorce will be even greater than that which was associated with their marriage. Thus, if there was ever any hope that they would be able to work effectively with one another in the future, the adversarial nature of the procedure they employ will tend to destroy that possibility forever.

There is another consideration that causes labor and management to avoid litigation and to turn instead to mediation. As everyone who has dealt with the courts and with our legal system knows, the law moves very slowly. In fact, it moves at a snail's pace. Particularly where the issues are complex and there is a great deal of preparation involved, it can often take a year or more before the issue will finally be presented to the court for its determination. Nor is that necessarily the end of it, as it can then take considerable time before a decision is rendered by the court. Even then the matter may not be at an end, as one of the parties may appeal the case, postponing its ultimate determination even longer.

There is only one problem, and that is that labor and management have to get on with the business of their lives. Nor can they wait forever while our judicial system takes its time to resolve the problems at hand. After all, what is the point of labor and management finally concluding their differences if the factory is no longer there for them to work in when they finally get through. If a resolution of their differences is going to be of any benefit to either of them, therefore, it has to be made expeditiously. And that means that other means have to be employed.

What is true of labor and management is equally true of separating and divorcing husbands and wives. Their decision to separate has undermined the very structure of their lives. As a result, it has left them, as well as the members of their immediate family, in a state of crisis. If they are going to re-establish order in their lives, and effectuate the necessary emotional closure with the past that they must, it is essential that the matters between them be put to rest expeditiously.

That is why those who voiced their concern over the very damaging effects that adversarial legal proceedings were having on the families involved began to explore the possibilities of mediation as an alternative. After all, if it worked successfully for so many others in our society, why could it not work as well for separating and divorcing couples? And this is why, beginning in the 1980s, more and more husbands and wives who found themselves faced with the prospect of divorce began to turn away from lawyers, and from adversarial legal proceedings, to divorce mediation.

What Is Divorce Mediation?

Divorce mediation is a procedure that helps married couples address, and successfully resolve, the problems they find themselves confronted with as a result of their decision to separate and divorce. It employs a neutral third person who will act as a facilitator of communication, and of the discussions between the parties, to the end that they will be able to answer the questions and make the decisions necessary for the two of them to conclude an agreement between themselves.

Divorce mediation proceeds on three main assumptions. The first is that it is Barbara and Bill themselves who are the experts in their lives. After all, it is they, and not their lawyers, who will have to live with whatever agreement they conclude. This being the case, they are the only ones who have a right to say whether it is acceptable or unacceptable.

The second assumption is that Barbara and Bill are stymied and need help, not because they have a legal problem, as lawyers would have it, but because they have lost the ability to do what they have always done in the past, without lawyers and without the intervention of third parties, namely, to sit down and decide the important issues in their lives based upon the considerations that were important to them, both individually and as a family. They have lost that ability because the very difficult feelings that one or both of them are struggling with have become encrusted around the practical problems that they are faced with and are making it difficult, and at times impossible, for them to deal with them effectively.

The third assumption is that if Barbara and Bill are given the right help and, more importantly, if that help is provided in the right setting, the ability they have lost can be restored to them and they will be able to conclude an agreement between themselves. It will be the mediator's job to provide them with that setting and with that assistance.

To conclude such an agreement, however, they will need five important things. The first thing they will need is a new set of ground rules. Unlike an adversarial legal proceeding, the object of divorce mediation is not to benefit one of them at the expense of the other. Nor is it to consider the needs of only Barbara or Bill and to leave the other wanting. To be sure, divorce lawyers may believe this, and then, to add insult to injury, may suggest that such a misguided pursuit represents responsible conduct; but divorce mediators, quite obviously, do not.

Divorce, after all, is not a game. It is a very serious business. Nor is the object for either Barbara or Bill to come out a winner and the other a loser. Again, divorce lawyers, who see it as legal warfare, may believe that, but it is not so, nevertheless. The object is to solve a problem that the two of them have in common, and that problem is to see to it that they are left with an agreement that they each feel they can live with. For, as divorce mediators know, it won't work for either Barbara or Bill unless it works for both of them.

The second thing that Barbara and Bill will need is a setting that will breed trust and not distrust—one that will tend to relieve their anxiety rather than intensify it further. Going through a divorce is frightening enough without having the discussions take place in a courtroom, or even in a lawyer's conference room. Nor does it help for them to take place between lawyers who view their role as legal gladiators, or to be conducted by a judge who, though he is a stranger to them, nevertheless has the power to make decisions binding upon them. Far better for Barbara and Bill to be assisted by someone who the two of them have chosen together and who they therefore feel is impartial. Far better for them to be assisted by someone who only has the power to help them and not the power to hurt them.

The third thing that Barbara and Bill will need is information. The object of mediation, after all, is to help the two of them make informed, intelligent decisions. To this end, they will need accurate information, not the exaggerated claims that adversarial lawyers will invariably induce each of them to make. Thus, if there is a question as to the value of Bill's business, the mediator is going to help them get the answer to that question from a single, impartial expert, and not, as would be the case in an adversarial proceeding, from two sets of accountants or appraisers who have been sent in to take adversarial positions and who come back with exaggerated evaluations that have no relationship to reality. Since neither Barbara nor Bill will feel that the impartial expert whom they have hired had any ax to grind or cause to serve, other than to give them an honest answer, they will be more likely to accept his opinion, even though it may vary from their expectations. And since they will receive that information in an atmosphere that will allow them to accept it, it will solve their problem rather than compound it.

The fourth thing that Barbara and Bill will need is guidance. While it may be true that the decisions they are faced with concern the same practical problems that they have always had to deal with in the past—their children, their home and the price of a new pair of shoes—nevertheless, they have never had to deal with those problem under these circumstances. In the past, they were only required to deal with them one at a time. Now, however, it is as if they are required to put their whole lives on the table. Suppose there is something one of them forgot to consider? Suppose there is something they overlooked? It will be the mediator's job to see that this does not happen and, just as importantly, to make them feel assured that it won't.

Finally, the atmosphere in which the mediation will take place, and the trust that they will each come to have in the mediator, will help Barbara and Bill deal more effectively with the difficult feelings that are so overwhelming them, feelings that are not only standing between them and an agreement but are making it so difficult for them to look forward to the future rather than back to the past. Going through a divorce is difficult at best. Nor can anyone else do it for them. Divorce lawyers, to be sure, sell their services by convincing Barbara and Bill that they can. But this, too, is simply legal mythology. If their problems are going to be solved, then the two of them will have to solve them. However, since the problems they are faced with are admittedly difficult ones, they are going to need help. That is what the mediator is there to give them.

The Initial Meeting

All divorce mediations start out with what is known as a "get to know you" meeting. The mediator does not assume that Barbara and Bill have decided to employ mediation, let alone his services. Rather, he assumes that they have a problem and that they are exploring the different ways that are available to them to deal with it. To be sure, they could attempt to discuss the issues on their own, but they know that, given the overwhelming feelings that one or both of them are struggling with, these discussions will probably be very painful and not particularly productive—that in most instances they will generate far more heat than light. Unfortunately, this doesn't leave them with too many options. Barbara and Bill know that they could go off and hire separate lawyers to conduct the discussions for them. But they have seen what has happened to friends and relatives who, having done that, became embroiled in adversarial legal proceedings, and they would like to avoid that. And so they have decided to explore the possibility of mediation.

The initial meeting that Barbara and Bill will have with the mediator will last between an hour and an hour-and-a-half. It will give the mediator an opportunity to explain the procedures he will follow and the issues they will address and to go over the materials that he will provide them with to assist them during the course of the mediation. It will also enable him to explain his role and the role of the advisory attorney with whom they will be working. In most instances, he will contrast divorce mediation with adversarial divorce proceedings, and emphasize the fact that, unlike a judge, he is not there to make the decisions in their lives. Rather, he is there to facilitate the discussions between them so that they can come to their own agreement.

The initial meeting will also give Barbara and Bill the opportunity to ask whatever questions they may have about the process as well as to discuss any concerns that they may have. One or both of them may have already spoken to friends or relatives, and not uncommonly to lawyers, who, in reinforcing legal mythology, have caused them to look distrustfully towards one another and made them fearful of employing mediation. The initial meeting will afford the mediator the occasion to discuss their concerns and, hopefully, allay whatever fears they may have. Most importantly, it will give the parties an opportunity to establish rapport with the mediator and to begin to build the relationship that is so important for its success. The mediator knows how difficult this is for them, and he is there because he wants to help them and because he believes that he knows how to help them. Hopefully, by the time the initial meeting is concluded, both Barbara and Bill will begin to sense this.

Following the initial meeting, and if Barbara and Bill both decide that they would like to employ the mediator's services, they will schedule further appointments with him for that purpose. As a rule, the mediator will prefer to meet with them once a week, for between an hour and an hour and a half. There are a number of reasons for this. The meetings are usually that length because the mediator wants Barbara and Bill to see some progress, and if they were shorter it would not give them enough time. On the other hand, the mediator does not like to schedule longer meetings because he does not want either Barbara or Bill to be worn down by what may seem to them as "marathon" sessions. While that is common practice in labor mediation, it is not in divorce mediation.

The spacing of the meetings also has a purpose. The mediator wants to have continuity in the process, and meeting on a weekly basis tends to serve that purpose. On the other hand, he also wants to have spaces between the meetings so that Barbara and Bill will be able to think about what has taken place and to digest it. The object, after all, is for the two of them to make informed, intelligent decisions, and they deserve the time that is necessary for that purpose. In that regard, the mediator has a luxury that adversarial lawyers do not have, and that is that the mediation is not going to take so long that he has to worry that, in spacing the meetings as he has, the mediation may take two or three weeks longer than it otherwise might. In fact, most mediations are concluded to the point where it is time to prepare a draft of the agreement that Barbara and Bill will ultimately sign in less time than it would have taken their separate attorneys just to complete the preparations necessary for the two of them to begin their negotiations.

In many instances, a mediator will get to this point in only a small fraction of that time.

Time and Money

As anyone who has dealt with lawyers knows, cost is a function of time. The more time it takes, the more money it costs. And as anyone who has gone through an adversarial divorce will tell you, it can cost a small fortune. In fact, the cost of getting a divorce in the United States today is nothing short of a national disgrace. Divorce lawyers may defend that cost by invoking the legal mythology that what is at issue are questions of great principle. And if it is a new principle, they will add the further justification that what they are doing is setting precedent. But by whatever name it is called, it is still legal highway robbery.

Cost is also a function of time in divorce mediation. However, there is one big difference, and that is that it will take only a fraction of the time. In fact, in most instances a couple will be able to conclude an agreement with the mediator's help in between six to eight sessions. Even if it should take longer, however, the time involved will still be only a fraction of what an adversarial proceeding would cost. As a result, the combined fee that a couple will pay to conclude a mediated agreement will generally be less than the retainer that either one of them would have had to ante up just to initiate an adversarial legal proceeding. And that retainer, of course, may only be a small fraction of their total fee.

Why is it that the cost of a completed mediation is so often less than either Barbara or Bill would have to pay their individual attorneys just as a down payment? And how is it possible for a mediator to conclude an agreement for them in such a short period of time? The answer is that it is not such a short period of time. It is just that all of the time that the mediator will devote to their matter, and charges them for, is productive time.

As we have seen, and because they have made it so difficult for Barbara and Bill to conclude an agreement, their attorneys will be required to spend many wasteful hours preparing and responding to pleadings, making and defending motions and appearing in court. Why are they wasteful? They are wasteful because in the overwhelming majority of instances they will have little, if any, effect upon the ultimate outcome. They are wasteful because it was only necessary to expend this time and effort because they did not have an agreement. Finally, they are wasteful because in most cases they will only further poison the atmosphere between Barbara and Bill, making it even more difficult for them to conclude an agreement. Nevertheless, the two of them will have to pay for that time anyway.

Let us give an example. As night follows day, almost every divorce action will be initiated, or quickly followed, by an application to the court for temporary maintenance and child support. This, as we have seen, is occasioned by the fact that Bill will not be encouraged by his attorney to give Barbara and their children what she really needs until they have concluded an agreement, or until the court has decided the case, and because Barbara's lawyer will not permit her to sit by and accept what Bill considers to be adequate. While this application will rarely result in a decision that either Barbara or Bill will applaud, it will cost them both dearly, nevertheless. In fact this one application could cost them as much as an entire mediation.

But won't they have this same problem in mediation? The answer is no. As we have seen, the setting in which mediation takes place is such that Bill will not feel that it is either necessary or appropriate for him to give Barbara less than she really needs, let alone to apply economic pressure to her to make her buckle under. Nor will it reward him if he does. For the same reason, he will not have cause to complain that Barbara is making it difficult for him to see his children as he would like. Except in the rarest of instances, this kind of conduct is simply not going to happen. However, even if Barbara or Bill should have a complaint, it is not going to take an application to court, which could take weeks and sometimes even months to decide, to resolve it. On the contrary, in most instances it will take but a few minutes of the mediator's time. And that is all the time that Barbara and Bill will be charged for.

Thus, if you were to compare the time records of a divorce lawyer and a divorce mediator, you would notice something very disturbing. Almost all of the mediator's time will have been spent in working out an agreement between the parties while very little, if any, of the lawyer's time will have been employed for that purpose. Is it any wonder, then, that divorce mediators are so successful in concluding agreements while divorce lawyers are not? And is it any wonder that the cost of an agreement concluded through mediation is so much less?

There is an important moral in this. By definition, Barbara and Bill are going to have serious problems in the future. They will therefore need every penny that they have. Nor can they afford to squander their money on long, pointless wars. The object, after all, is to save their money to put their own children through college, not to use it to put their attorneys' children through college. Divorce lawyers may not understand this, but it is true, nevertheless.

Divorce lawyers, after all, are simply legal undertakers. They bury dead marriages. While funerals should be conducted with dignity, it makes absolutely no sense for Barbara and Bill to dig a deep hole and to throw their hard-earned dollars into it. On the contrary, it should cost no more than dignity requires.

The Quality of the Agreement

Ironically, although a divorce mediation is usually completed in only a fraction of the time that it would take to conclude the same matter by means of adversarial legal proceedings, the parties will invariably be left with a better and more complete agreement.

Why is this? It is easy to understand why the agreement will be better. It will be better because it will attempt to meet the needs of both Barbara and Bill, not just the needs of one of them—better, because it will be an agreement that each of them feels they can live with. But how can an attorney say that the agreement that he will conclude for Barbara and Bill in mediation will be a more complete agreement than the agreement that their own attorneys will conclude in an adversarial proceeding?

The mythology, again, is that the adversarial nature of those proceedings is intended to assure that nothing is overlooked, as it is each lawyer's function to check up on the other. Thus, as two minds are better than one, so, too, two adversarial lawyers are better than the single advisory attorney with whom the couple will be working in divorce mediation. That might be true if the two lawyers were working together toward the same end. But they are not. They are working at cross purposes.

As we have seen, the very nature of our adversarial legal system will make it more difficult rather than less difficult for Barbara and Bill to conclude an agreement. That is because they have been given such conflicting opinions, and therefore different expectations, by their separate lawyers. To get them to an agreement—any agreement—is therefore going to be extremely difficult. To leave them with the agreement they have each been promised would require a miracle. But since their lawyers do not have magic wands, they will not be able to give them such an agreement. And therein lies the problem.

Let us explain this. Mediators have an expression that a dispute between a separated and divorce couple is simply a question that their agreement didn't answer. Thus, in a year from now, if either Barbara or Bill has a question, they should be able to open their agreement and find the answer or, if that is not possible, then at least to find the procedure that they are to follow in order to get that answer. One of them may be slightly disappointed, but that is what they agreed to and so there will be no dispute.

Isn't that the kind of agreement that Barbara and Bill will be left with in an adversarial proceeding, having had the benefit of two attorneys rather than one? The answer, ironically, is no. Why is this? Because their two attorneys, in giving them such different answers to the same questions—such different levels of expectation—have made it difficult enough for themselves without adding to their problems. The result is that they cannot afford to raise all of the questions they would like to—all of the questions that should be answered in Barbara's and Bill's agreement—and they hope that the other attorney with whom they are dealing will be smart enough not to raise them either.

Let us give an example of this. Finally, and after many months, and sometimes not until they actually get to the courthouse steps, Barbara's and Bill's attorneys have reached an agreement on the question of support. Since it is so much less than Barbara was led to believe she was entitled to receive, and so much more than Bill was led to believe he was obligated to give to her, neither of them is very happy. But at least they have an agreement. There is only one problem. Even if the amount of support that they have agreed to is adequate today, that does not mean that it will be adequate tomorrow. Suppose that the cost of living goes up. Suppose that there is a substantial increase in Bill's income, or in Barbara's for that matter. And what if either of them should suffer severe financial reverses, or the needs of their children should increase? Certainly their agreement will take these possibilities into consideration. Certainly the safeguards of our adversarial legal system will assure that these questions will be raised and answered.

It would be a serious mistake to bet on it; as the odds are that they will not. As we have seen, it was hard enough for Barbara's and Bill's attorneys to get them to an agreement as to what the payment would be today. In fact, it undoubtedly took them many months, and in some instances a year or more, to do that. To attempt to gild the lily by worrying about what the payment should be tomorrow is, unfortunately, a luxury that our adversarial legal system cannot afford. Thus, neither attorney will raise the question himself, and each will hope that the other is smart enough not to raise it either. That is just one of the many prices of adversarial legal proceedings, and the less said about it the better.

But doesn't that expose Barbara's and Bill's attorneys to risk? Perhaps, but not to as much risk as they would subject themselves to were they to raise the issue. Why is that? Because if Barbara's lawyer raises the question of a cost-of-living increase he has not only put the issue on the table himself, he has now also educated Barbara as to its importance. But suppose that Bill's lawyer will not agree to it—and you can bet that he won't. Where does that leave Barbara's attorney? It leaves him with a problem, because he will either be left with no agreement at all or with one that he has already impliedly suggested to Barbara that she cannot afford to sign. And that will not do. It may have been alright to fill Barbara's head with false levels of expectation in the salad days when he was trying to impress her. But these are now the dog days and he, too, would like to get it done—not uncommonly because the parties are financially, even if not personally, exhausted. And so he decides that, all things considered—and one of the things he now has to consider is the risk that he may not get paid for the work that he will have to do if the matter is not settled at this point—it is best to say nothing. And, for the same reason, Bill's lawyer says nothing either.

What is acceptable in adversarial practice is not acceptable in mediation, however. In part, this is because the goals of the two procedures are so different. Divorce lawyers will hand Barbara and Bill a piece of paper and tell them that they are divorced. But as a piece of paper did not their marriage make, so, too, a piece of paper will not their divorce make. Thus, all their lawyers will have given them will be a legal divorce, not an emotional one. Worse yet, and by subjecting them to adversarial divorce proceedings, they will have made any hope of an emotional divorce all but impossible. Divorce lawyers know this. In fact, they have an expression for it. This expression is that divorces never end. What they do not realize, unfortunately, is that it is the very procedures they have employed that will assure that they never end, for by leaving Barbara and Bill as hurt and angry when they get through as they were when they began, they will all but guarantee that the in-fighting will continue, with children and money being the most common weapons.

Understandably, divorce mediators want to leave Barbara and Bill with more than just a legal divorce. They also want to help them effectuate some emotional closure to the difficult feelings that they are struggling with—to help them to effectuate an emotional divorce as well. It will not do, therefore, to send them off with the illusion of an agreement but without the reality of one, as is so often the case when they conclude an agreement through the use of adversarial proceedings. If they are to effectuate an emotional divorce, they must be left with a complete agreement and not just with half of one. That is why mediators raise all the important questions, not just some of them.

To be sure, many of these questions are hard ones—that is why it is so important that they be raised. But they are not make-or-break questions, as adversarial lawyers assume. They are only make-or-break questions in the context in which all of the questions that Barbara and Bill must answer are dealt with in the adversarial world of the law. Those questions may be difficult, but as countless couples who have turned to divorce mediation have learned, they can be asked and answered in the right context, and with the right help.

The belief that two adversarial lawyers are better than

the one advisory attorney that Barbara and Bill will work with in mediation is thus also simply legal mythology. As we have seen, just the opposite is the case. But there is an even greater irony in this. For while Barbara's and Bill's separate lawyers will, almost without exception, discourage them from employing mediation in an effort to conclude an agreement, their divorce mediator, on the other hand, will afford them every opportunity to consult with their own lawyers should they choose to do that.

A divorce mediator, after all, wants to help Barbara and Bill to make informed, intelligent decisions. Moreover, he wants to help them to conclude an agreement that they will be able to live with tomorrow, not just one that they feel they can live with today. And he will leave no stone unturned in his effort to do that.

In turning to divorce mediation, therefore, Barbara and Bill can have the best of both worlds. Thus, while adversarial lawyers will almost always discourage Barbara and Bill from turning to a mediator, their mediator's attitude will be just the opposite. Thus, if they wish to consult with separate lawyers, and if their separate lawyers have something constructive to contribute, he will not only listen to their advice and opinion. He will welcome it.

Suppose the Mediation Goes Wrong

Divorce lawyers will do more than discourage Barbara and Bill from employing mediation. They will put the fear of God into them. How will they do that? They will do it by telling them war stories. Barbara's lawyer will tell her about the woman who was ripped off in mediation, and Bill's lawyer will tell him about the man who ended up paying through the nose. And they will both ask them how their rights will be protected if they are not there to do the protecting. In short, they will tell them fairy tales that will play to their fears, since that is what sells.

But don't Barbara and Bill have something to fear, and

shouldn't they worry about what may happen to them in mediation? The answer is no. In fact, nothing could be farther from the truth, and it is again only legal mythology that they do. A mediator, after all, does not make any decisions. His job is not to hear Barbara out and then to hear Bill out and then to give his own opinion. That is what a judge does. All that he is there to do is help Barbara and Bill to conclude their own agreement.

If a mediator does not make any decisions, then he has no power. Moreover, if he has no power, then Barbara and Bill have it all. And if they have it all, then they do not have to worry. For if the mediation should go in a direction that they did not expect, or if their worst fears should come to pass, since they have all the power in the world, all that they have to do to stop it is to stand up and leave. And that is the best protection of all.

Ironically, again, it is an adversarial proceeding, and the power that a judge has that a mediator does not, that Barbara and Bill should most fear. For if the proceeding should go in a direction that either of them did not expect, or if their worst fears should come to pass, since the judge has all of the power and they none, there will be nothing that either of them can do. Nor can they just get up and leave. In an adversarial proceeding, no one leaves until the judge gives him permission to do so.

There is an important lesson in this. Contrary to legal mythology, and contrary to the parade of possible horrors that Barbara's and Bill's lawyers will spread before them, if there is really something so wonderful to be had in lawyer-land, and if either Barbara or Bill do not receive it in mediation, they are each free to leave. Nor will they have to wait months or years to find out. They will know in but a matter of weeks. This is one of the great virtues of mediation. It won't cost a king's ransom, it won't take forever and it won't force either Barbara or Bill to do anything that they are not willing to do.

THE TWELFTH MYTH

Separating and Divorcing Couples
Get Exactly What They Deserve

Most responsible divorce lawyers know that our adversarial system does great damage to separating and divorcing couples. They also know that it does even more damage, and very often permanent damage, to their children. Nor are they oblivious to the fact that, in participating in that system, they are contributing to the injury that all parties suffer.

This raises a question. If lawyers know that they are aiding and abetting a process that is as destructive as it is, why do they participate in it? More importantly, how do they explain it to themselves?

The answer, unfortunately, will not be very satisfactory. Nor will it be particularly flattering to the legal profession. As we have seen, most divorce lawyers, having bought the same legal mythology that they sell to their clients, really believe that what they are engaged in is a holy crusade, doing God's work. Thus, and just as generals who send our young men and women off to do battle in foreign lands do not talk about death and destruction, but instead about freedom and democracy, so, too, attorneys who send husbands and wives off to do battle with one another in lawyer-land do not talk about human suffering and crippling emotional injury. Rather, they talk about rights and justice, and about what is fair and equitable.

But what about the cost involved: not only the cost in terms of time and money but, and more importantly, the terrible personal cost? Unfortunately, and since the very purpose of invoking these abstractions is to mute that question, it rarely, if ever, gets asked. After all, everything has a price, and if it is important enough, then it is worth paying for. Besides, it is not for Barbara's or Bill's lawyers to decide whether what they want is worth the price that they will have to pay to get it. It is for them to decide, and if they feel that it isn't worth the price, then they won't pay it. In short, divorce lawyers do not answer the question for the very simple reason that they refuse to acknowledge that it is their problem.

For more responsible attorneys, however, it is not that easy. It may be that everything has its price. Nevertheless, on some level at least, they know that they are still left with blood on their hands. Thus, they feel the need to offer some answer. Unfortunately, and although they are themselves responsible, the answers that they proffer up are not. Nor will they do.

The first answer that they will give is that they are simply lawyers. Thus, when it was suggested to a divorce lawyer that she was not helping the problem, but only adding to it, she indignantly replied, "I don't make things worse. I am just a legal technician."

What did she mean by this? What she meant, and more importantly as what she was doing proved, was absolving herself of all responsibility. She was a legal mathematician who had been trained to add and subtract legal numbers— to apply legal principles. Her job was to employ them correctly, to the best of her ability. However, she was not responsible for how they added up. Nor was she responsible for whether their application led to a desirable conclusion or an undesirable one, or even whether they helped. After all, she did not make the rules, she only applied them.

That answer may suffice for mathematicians. It will not do for lawyers, however. In fact, and as history all too clearly demonstrates, the idea that technicians are only responsible for the proper application of their technique, but not to the ends to which their skill is applied, is an extremely dangerous one. All of us are accountable for the consequences of our actions. This, after all, is what it means to be responsible. Thus, if the application of legal rules and principles invariably makes things more difficult, rather than less difficult, for separating and divorcing husbands and wives, and for their children, then lawyers are charged with that knowledge. Nor can they avoid their responsibility by pleading that they are simply legal technicians.

The answer is wanting for yet another reason. Lawyers are not, like mathematicians, just applying abstract legal principles. They have also become advocates in their clients cause. As we have seen, a mathematician could not care less what the outcome of his efforts is, or whether it pleases or displeases the person who has given him the problem to solve. This is why he can honestly say that he is simply applying mathematical rules and that he is not responsible for their outcome.

A divorce lawyer, on the other hand, is very interested in the outcome. In fact, his job is not to dispassionately apply legal principles to the end that they will produce whatever result they may. Rather, and as we have seen, it is to manipulate those legal rules so that they will produce the result that his client desires, for that is what he was hired to do. Divorce lawyers are thus more than mere legal technicains. They are allies in their clients' cause and, therefore, accomplices to their purposes.

There is one final difficulty with this answer. Mathematicians, after all, apply mathematical principles because they have no choice—because there is no other way to come up with an answer. Lawyers, however, do have a choice. There is no law that says that they must commit Barbara and Bill to do legal combat with one another in order for them to conclude an agreement. They do not even have to insist that they conclude one by the application of legal rules— which, after all, embody abstract principles having little, if anything, to do with the reality of their lives. They could sit them down together and help them mediate their differences. Thus, if they commit them to adversarial legal proceedings—to a process where legal rules and principles will be used by each of them as weapons to get as much as they can and to give as little as they have to—it is because they choose to do that, not because they have to. That being so, they are responsible for that choice and, with it, for its consequences.

Most divorce lawyers will answer the question differently. Again, and particularly if they are responsible, they will not deny the fact that adversarial divorce proceedings are very destructive. At times, they may even go further and acknowledge that, like all wars, they are nothing short of insane. But they will not take responsibility for that insanity, nevertheless. How will they avoid it? They will blame it on Barbara and Bill.

But aren't Barbara and Bill to blame? After all, who is it who lies about his income and gives Barbara less than she and their children need, if it is not Bill? And who is it who exaggerates her needs, prevents Bill from seeing his children as often as he would like and bad-mouths him to his business associates, if it is not Barbara? And who is it who poison their children's minds, if it is not the two of them? It was not their lawyers who told them to divorce one another. Nor did their lawyers cause them to feel as bitterly towards one another as they do. They did all of that long before their lawyers came on the scene. Why, then, are their lawyers responsible for how they act towards one another, or towards their children, for that matter? Their lawyers are responsible because, and whether wittingly or unwittingly, they are aiding and abetting the process.

When Barbara's and Bill's attorneys renounce all responsibility for the casualties that take place in divorce wars, they are falling back on the canard that there is nothing unique in the way that Barbara and Bill are acting. Quite the contrary, it is to be expected. This is the way that all separating and divorcing couples act. If you do not believe this, ask any matrimonial attorney and he will tell you that it is so.

There is only one problem. If you ask any divorce mediator you will get a very different answer. To be sure, divorce lawyers spend their lives in the never ending battle of attempting to put out the brush fires caused by the misconduct of divorcing husbands or wives. But that is not what divorce mediators do. They help those same couples conclude agreements between themselves. But won't Barbara come in complaining that she has just received a letter from the utility company threatening to terminate her services? And won't Bill come in complaining that when he went to pick up his children the previous Friday, as he and Barbara had discussed, that night neither Barbara nor they were there. After all, that is what their lawyers will hear from them, ad nauseam. For that is the conduct that all divorcing husbands and wives engage in. Contrary to legal mythology, however, it is not. It is only the conduct they engage in when they turn to adversarial proceedings. If you don't believe this, ask any mediator and he will tell you that it is so.

Legal mythology notwithstanding, the conduct that lawyers bear witness to is not a by-product of divorce, as they summarily assume. As we have already seen, it is only a by-product of adversarial divorce proceedings. To be sure, if you throw Barbara and Bill into a life-and-death struggle, and then tell them that only one of them will come out a survivor, it will not be long before each of them will begin to act in ways that, even by their own standards, are less than appropriate. If you work at it, you can even get them to act like animals. But that does not mean that they are really animals. It only means that, like every self-fulfilling prophesy, in persuading them that they are enemies they will soon begin to act as if they are.

It will not do, therefore, for divorce lawyers to exonerate themselves of all responsibility and to lay the blame at Barbara's and Bill's feet. It will not do, in other words, for lawyers to organize divorce as a three-ring circus and then complain that Barbara and Bill are acting like clowns. On the contrary, they must bear the heavy burden of that blame themselves.

To be sure, there is much hurt and anger that both Barbara and Bill are experiencing. It is also true that each of them will tend to direct their feelings at the other as having been responsible for them. But this still leaves a choice. We can recommend that they attempt to resolve their problems in a setting that, in tending to confirm the validity of their feelings, will only exacerbate them further. Or we can recommend that they turn, instead, to a setting conducive to just the opposite. Those who counsel Barbara and Bill are responsible for the choices they recommend, as they are responsible for the consequences of those choices. Nor can they avoid that responsibility by laying it on Barbara and Bill.

To be sure, this may be true of Barbara and Bill. After all, while, like the rest of us, they obviously have their faults, they are still basically decent people. But what about those husbands and wives who are not? Certainly they didn't need any help from their attorneys to do all the injury that they did.

In fairness, no one who has been involved with divorce can deny that there are people like this—people who, though they may be finished with their husbands and wives, are not, nevertheless, done with them. And these are the people whom divorce lawyers, even responsible divorce lawyers, will point to in support of their argument. In fact, it is these people who will make up their entire defense.

Unfortunately, there are a number of problems with this argument. To begin with, it ignores Barbara and Bill, who are the rule, and not the exception that divorce lawyers point to. They are basically decent people, not the highly disturbed and distorted husbands and wives that divorce lawyers bring forward as material witnesses in their defense. And yet our adversarial legal system has made criminals of them as well. To be sure, theirs may not be the high crimes that some divorcing husbands and wives are guilty of. Nevertheless, they are not crimes that they would have committed if they had been given another choice. Again, if proof of this is necessary, it will be found, as we have seen, in the fact that they will not be guilty of any of those crimes when they turn, instead, to mediation.

But what about those husbands and wives who are not Barbara and Bill? In fact, what about those husbands and wives who act little better than common criminals and who will do their dirty work to one another no matter what? Divorce mediation, so adversarial lawyers will maintain, is a self-selective process. As a result, mediators do not see husbands and wives such as this.

Contrary to legal mythology, divorce mediation is not quite the self-selective system that lawyers contend that it is, and many people such as this do find their way to a mediator's door. To be sure, a mediator will be far less effective, and perhaps not effective at all, with people such as this. But nor will the adversarial procedures that divorce lawyers apply. On the contrary, and ironically, our adversarial system will reward these people the most.

As we have seen, adversarial divorce proceedings represent a kind of institutionalized madness. As in all wars, each of the parties is required to engage in conduct that would otherwise be considered irrational. To get husbands and wives to do this, and to accept it as appropriate, it is first necessary to give it official sanction, and that is the purpose of legal mythology. The healthier a person is, however, the more he will realize just how crazy what he is involved in is, and the damage it is doing to everyone around him. To end this madness, he will be willing to make concessions and compromises. In fact, it is because he is basically emotionally healthy that he is willing and able to do this.

For the less healthy people in society, however, just the opposite is the case. For them it is more important to be right and to get even than it is to get done and get on. Nor does it make any difference what the price will be, or the injury that will be inflicted, to their spouse, to their children, or even to themselves for that matter. They are involved in a holy crusade, and they will see it through to the end, regardless of the price, for whatever the cost, it can never be too great. Again, it is because they are basically so unhealthy that they are willing and able to do this.

A fine system it is that rewards the least healthy element in society, and puts those of us who are more healthy at a disadvantage. A fine system it is that will take Barbara and Bill and get them to act in ways that are no better. A sad day it is when the champions of that system, and those who administer it, turn their backs on all of the dirty work that is done and, disclaiming any responsibility for it, simply blame it on Barbara and BIll.

Get It Right/Get It in Writing

If others are responsible for the options they recommend to Barbara and Bill, the two of them, nevertheless, are responsible for the options they choose. Nor will it do for them to attempt to renounce that responsibility and to blame it on their lawyers.

Barbara and Bill know what will happen to them if they run off to lawyers and to lawyer-land to do legal battle with one another. They have seen what has happened to friends and relatives who did. When they began, their divorce was already a terrible misfortune. By the time they got done, it had become a living nightmare.

To be sure, Barbara and Bill will each blame that nightmare on the other. In fact, one of the ways that their lawyers will avoid their own responsibility for what will happen will be to encourage them in this belief. And since it will be impossible for either of them to see how they have contributed to the tragedy that will have taken place—each of them will simply see what the other has done and will view their own conduct as an understandable, if not appropriate, response to that—each of them will see themselves as being blameless, as they were blameless for their divorce itself. In short, when they get through, they will have proved their attorneys were right. It is not their divorce that is the problem. The problem is their husband or wife.

If the stakes are as high as they are, and if the consequences are so potentially damaging, neither Barbara nor Bill can afford to leap before they look. Nor can they allow their emotions to get the better of them, or their fear to cause them to panic, for if they do, they will pay for it dearly. The price that their children will pay may even be greater. Rather, they must remember that if they do not take control of the events in their lives, the events in their lives will take control of them.

Before Barbara and Bill buy legal mythology, therefore, and turn their lives over to lawyers, they ought to ask a few questions. Not just of themselves, but of their attorneys as well. More importantly, they ought to get those answers in writing. After all, talk is cheap, and vague talk is even cheaper. Therefore, if their lawyers promise them the sun, the stars and the moon, they ought to get a clear picture of what they look like. To be exact, they ought to insist that the lawyers who are so anxious to take their case tell them, specifically, exactly what they can expect to get if they retain their services. And they should also find out exactly what the cost of those services will be.

Is that a fair question for Barbara and Bill to ask their attorneys? It is and it isn't. Just as an economist cannot tell us exactly how much the cost of living will increase in the next twelve months—whether it will increase 4.2 percent or 5.7 percent—so, too, even the most experienced divorce lawyer can not tell Barbara whether the maintenance she will receive from Bill will be $400 a week or $450 a week, let alone exactly how long she will receive it. It is simply impossible for him to know. In that sense, then, it is not a fair question.

When, then, is it a fair question? It is a fair question

when that same attorney makes promises to Barbara that he cannot keep—when he promises her that the cost of living will not increase more than 4.2 percent in the next twelve months or that she will receive maintenance of at least $450 a week for at least ten years, when he could not possibly know this. In other words, if he is willing to play on Barbara's fears and to give her grand assurances in order to get her business, then she has a right to ask that he put it in writing. After all, as he will expect the check that Barbara gives him as a retainer to be honored by her bank, so, too, Barbara has the right to expect that he will honor his commitment to her. And as he wants her commitment to be in writing, and to be paid up front, she has a right to ask for the same thing. In other words, unless he is prepared to be absolutely honest and tell Barbara that he really does not know how much maintenace she will receive, and for how long, then he should be expected to put his money where his mouth is. Barbara should get a letter stating what it is that she will receive with an understanding that her money will be returned to her if she does not.

To be sure, no lawyer will give Barbara such a letter. Nor will he give her any such assurance, let alone put it in writing. Instead, he will excuse himself by saying that it is not possible for him to tell Barbara exactly what the outcome will be, and then lapse into a colloquy filled with vague references and assurances whose principal purpose it will be to avoid the question rather than to answer it. After all, as an economist cannot tell Barbara whether the cost of living will increase 4.2 percent or 5.7 percent in the next twelve months, so, too, an attorney cannot tell Barbara how much she will receive in support or for how long. All that he can tell her is that he will try to get her as much as he can, and that is what she is paying him for.

Before Barbara accepts these vague promises as substitute for hard currency—and before she turns over her hard-earned money in exchange for such vague promises—it would pay for her to examine his answer a little more closely. To be sure, even an expert economist may not be able to tell her exactly how much the cost of living will go up in the next twelve months. But he should be able to give her some idea—that it will go up no less than 2 percent and no more than 7 percent. And if can't even do that, then what right does he have to call himself an expert economist? More importantly, if he can't do that, why would we waste our time or money asking him his opinion?

Thus, if Barbara truly wants to test out what the lawyer she is considering retaining is really telling her, and how much of what he is saying she can actually rely on, she should pose him the following question. And she should not take no for an answer. After having heard him tell her what she can expect and for how long, she should write the answers in two columns. Let us say that she has been left with the impression that she will receive maintenance of between $425 and $450 a week for approximately nine or ten years. Acknowledging that she knows that these are only estimates on his part, and that she appreciates that he cannot give her an exact answer, she has made the following chart that she would like him to take a look at.

Table 12.1   Sample Maintenance Chart

$200	1 year
$225	2 years
$250	3 years
$275	4 years
$300	5 years
$325	6 years
$350	7 years
$375	8 years
$400	9 years
$425	10 years

What Barbara should now ask him to do is to circle the number in the left column that represents the lowest amount that he is willing to assure her, in writing, that she will receive. (If this is Bill asking the question, what he would like his lawyer to do is to circle the number in that same column that represents the highest amount that he is willing to assure him, again in writing, that he will be obligated to pay.)

In both instances, Barbara and Bill should also ask their attorneys to circle the number in the right column representing the least number of years (in the case of Barbara) or the most number of years (in the case of Bill) that the maintenance will continue.

Let us assume that after some urging—and it will take more than some urging on Barbara's part—her attorney circles the numbers $250 and five years. What that should tell Barbara is that in his opinion it is possible that she may only receive maintenance of $250 a week for no more than five years. To be sure, it is possible that she may come away with more. But that is the most that he is willing to guarantee her.

There is something else that Barbara and Bill should find out, and that is how much it is going to cost them to get this. Again, they should take the estimate that their lawyer has given them as to his fees and make a chart with that amount at the top. They should then increase that fee, nine times, by an amount, in each instance, equal to his retainer. (Let us assume that Barbara's attorney has told her that his retainer is $2,000 and that he estimates that his total fee will be no more than $5,000. Her chart would then be $5,000, $7,000, $9,000, and so forth.) What Barbara should then ask him to do is to circle the number that represents the highest amount that he is willing to assure her, again in writing, that she will be obligated to pay him.

Should Barbara or Bill feel uncomfortable that they have put their attorneys on the spot in asking them to do this? The answer is no. It is a perfectly fair question. It is only the answer that may prove embarrassing. But they shouldn't feel uncomfortable for another reason, and that is that their attorneys aren't going to answer either of these questions. They are going to wiggle out of them again. They refused to give them a guarantee as to how much they would receive or be required to pay because they knew that they really didn't and couldn't know that. They will now refuse to tell Barbara and Bill how much it may cost them because they don't want them to know that.

If that is the case, what is the point of the question? The point is that if Barbara and Bill are smart, they can learn as much, and more, from the questions that their attorneys are unwilling to answer as they can from those that they are. They went to their attorneys, after all, because they were looking for answers. What they learned, if they listened carefully, is that there are no answers, and that their attorneys did not really promise them anything definite. What did they promise them then? All that they promised them was that they would fight as hard for them as they could. And therein lies the rub. They consulted with their attorneys in order to get answers. They did not come away with any answers, however. On the contrary, all that they came away with was the assurance that they would get a good fight.

Before either Barbara or Bill engages in this fight, however, there is one more thing that they should do. In fact, if either of them is still holding on to any shred of legal mythology, it is guaranteed to dispel it. Husbands and wives buy legal mythology, as we have seen, because it plays to their fears. But they also buy it for a less obvious reason, and that is that they are only told half the story. They might well have second thoughts, however, were they to hear it all. And that is what they should do.

Barbara and Bill should each make appointments to consult with separate attorneys. However, since they want to hear the whole story and not just half of it, they must go, not alone, but together. If they announce that they are husband and wife, of course, it will not work. In fact, neither of their attorneys will be willing to meet with them together. So what they must do is pose as brother and sister. Barbara should tell her attorney that, for emotional support, she has asked her brother, Bill, to come with her and she would very much like him to sit in on the meeting. In that way, if she should not hear everything or forget something—and because she is so upset that is a very real possibility—he will be able to remember it for her. And Bill, of course, will tell his attorney the same thing. There is one rule that they must follow very strictly, however. Neither of them may say anything or ask any questions during the other's consultation. All that they may do is sit politely and listen.

It is not going to be very pleasant. In fact, when Barbara and Bill get through, both of them will have second thoughts about retaining the attorneys with whom they have consulted. Instead, they will run off and hire the first mediator whom they can find. After all, it is one thing to sit there and hear how your legal champion is going to protect you and what he is going to do to your husband or wife. It is quite another thing, as they will find, to sit there and hear what your husband's or wife's legal champion intends to do to you. Nor will Barbara or Bill be particularly pleased by the colorful, and all too often less-than-flattering, language that the other's attorney may use to describe him or her, let alone the advice that he may give to their spouse as to how he or she should prepare himself or herself for the battle ahead. In short, if Barbara and Bill want to get an accurate picture of what is in store for the two of them, it is not enough to look at the pretty pictures that their own attorneys will paint. They must also look at the ugly pictures that the other's attorney will create.

CONCLUSION

Barbara and Bill deserve better than they will get from lawyers and from our adversarial legal system. All separating and divorcing couples deserve better than they will get.

As we have seen, the lawyers to whom they will turn for help will not respond to the terrible tragedy that their divorce represents. Rather, they will simply use them as pawns in the game of legal chess that they will play with their lives. Nor will they concern themselves with how long it will take to play the game or how high the stakes may get before it is finally concluded. Rather, and when all else fails, they will justify it, and dismiss all concern, by falling back on the most pernicious legal myth of all. They are lawyers, and it is in playing the game of legal chess that they play with people's lives that legal precedents are established and justice is advanced.

Separating and divorcing couples do not want to establish legal precedent or make legal history, however. Nor should they be required to do this as the price for being able to get on with the important business of their lives. They are at a point of great crisis in their personal lives and what they want, and desparately need, is help. It is simply irresponsible to give them anything less.

Unfortunately, we have for so long accepted an adversarial legal system that advances legal principles by using human beings as legal guinea pigs, that we are no longer able to see just how inappropriate it is, let alone to question the heavy price that separating and divorcing couples are asked to pay in the process. We are not even able to see this despite the fact that we would never permit medical science, or any other discipline for that matter, to be advanced by allowing it to use human beings in the same manner. Nor would we allow all of the high sounding principles in the world to change our minds.

If this terrible human sacrifice is ever to end, we will first have to see legal mythology and legal hypocrisy for what they are. We will first have to reject all of the high sounding abstractions—justice and equity, and legal rights—that are used by lawyers to get separating and divorcing couples to march off to do legal battle with one another. But most importantly, we will first have to restore our ability to see divorce as being not a legal problem in these couples' lives but a serious personal problem. For it is only then that we will truly be able to help them as they deserve. It is only then that we will see that to be of help means to restore to them the ability that they have lost, namely, to sit down and to decide the important issues in their lives on their own. It is only then that we will reject either a coin, a foot race or a game of legal chess as an appropriate substitute for the one sane, sensible procedure that they should employ. It is called divorce mediation.

ABOUT THE AUTHOR

Lenard Marlow, who holds a B.A. in philosophy from Colgate University, received his legal education at the Columbia University School of Law. A Fellow of the American Academy of Matrimonial Lawyers and Past-President of the New York State Council on Divorce Mediation, Mr. Marlow was for many years President of the Board of Directors of the Pederson-Krag Center, one of the largest outpatient mental health facilities in New York state. Mr. Marlow, who is co-author with S. Richard Sauber, Ph.D., of *The Handbook of Divorce Mediation,* is the founder and director of legal services of Divorce Mediation Professionals, one of the oldest divorce mediation facilities in the United States. Mr. Marlow and his wife Marilyn have two children and live in Huntington, New York.

INDEX